living Legacy

Reflections on Dawson Trotman and Lorne Sanny

By Jim Downing

dawsonmedia®

P.O. Box 6000, Colorado Springs, CO 80934

A MINISTRY OF THE NAVIGATORS

Living Legacy: Reflections on Dawson Trotman and Lorne Sanny
By Jim Downing
© 2007 by Jim Downing. All rights reserved.

Published by

dawsonmedia®

a ministry of The Navigators
P.O. Box 6000, Colorado Springs, CO 80934

Editor: Leura Jones
Designer: Steve Learned

The Navigators is called to advance the Gospel of Jesus and His Kingdom into the nations through spiritual generations of laborers living and discipling among the lost.

Dawson Media is a ministry of The Navigators, dedicated to walking alongside disciples of Jesus Christ—helping them experiment with fresh and relevant tools for ministry.

Printed in the United States of America.

ISBN: 978-0-9729023-8-0

www.dawsonmedia.com

Dedication

This book is dedicated to the family of Dawson Trotman: Bruce, Ruth, who is in heaven with her parents, Burke, and Faith, and to Lucy Sanny and the Sanny children, Tom, Beverly, Cheryl, Charles, Jean, and Judy.

Contents

Foreword

IN NOVEMBER OF 1966, DURING MY FIRST YEAR at university in England, a fellow student invited me to the house of a Navigator staff couple who had just begun a ministry on our campus. Drawn by the qualities I observed in the life of my friend, I accepted his invitation. That evening changed the direction of my life. An American Navigator missionary spoke from the Bible in a way that was attractive and made sense to me. A young businessman from London shared how his faith in Christ was making a difference in his life. Later in the evening, another young businessman who was sitting next to me asked about my own faith journey. As I raised questions, he answered them from the Bible, helping me understand what Jesus had done for me on the cross and pointing out my need to make a clear faith response. That night after the meeting, standing alone on a street, I prayed, accepting for myself what Christ had done for me, drinking in His mercy and forgiveness for failures of which I was deeply aware, and asking for His help to begin to live for Him.

In the days that followed, I received a great deal of help and encouragement from my new Navigator friends. I began reading the Bible with a hunger I had never before experienced. I started to memorize Bible verses, reflecting on them in ways that began to change my attitudes, my thinking, and my life. I also began to ask: Who were these Navigators—the people from whom I was receiving so much encouragement and help? I remember listening with fascination to the stories about Dawson Trotman and the early Navigators. I soon realized that these were not adherents to some strange American sect but ordinary Christian men and women from many different Christian traditions, drawn together by a simple desire "to know Christ and to make Him known."

Those life-changing, first encounters with Navigators deepened and matured into lifelong friendships and a thrilling partnership in advancing the good news of Jesus into the nations. My interest in the faith and vision of the first Navigators has grown into a deep awareness of indebtedness and a sense of awe in the wonderful way God multiplies the faith influence of those who believe and follow Him wholeheartedly.

No one is better placed to recall for us the exploits of those early Navigators than Jim Downing. Jim was there almost from the start of Dawson's world-impacting encounter with Lester Spencer and his friends aboard the USS *West Virginia*.

I never had the privilege of meeting Daws. In fact, my first encounter with Navigators came 10 years after his death. Jim's engaging recollections bring Daws to life for me in ways that nothing else has. In Jim's book, I meet a man very different from me. I wonder how I would have responded had I met him in person. Here is the man who in some way is my great-great-great-grandfather spiritually, whose faith and vision have impacted me so deeply. As I read about him, I am filled with gratitude to God's grace expressed through this very human being whose love for Christ ignited a fire in so many lives.

I did have the privilege of knowing Lorne Sanny. Though I never worked closely with Lorne, I heard him speak many times, and I treasure the memories of several long, personal conversations—one of them just a few days before he died, when he prayed with me for the Lord's anointing on my own leadership of The Navigators.

I remember Lorne speaking on Hebrews 13:7, "Remember your leaders, who spoke the word of God to you. Consider the outcome of their way of life and imitate their faith" (NIV). For all of us whose lives have been touched in some way by the Navigator movement, reading Jim's book is a great way to follow this exhortation to *remember* and *consider*. May the Lord also help us *imitate their faith.*

Whether or not you are a Navigator—even if you had never before heard of The Navigators until you picked up this book—Jim Downing's narrative will give you reason to marvel at the wonderful way that God in His grace and mercy takes the lives of ordinary people and makes them channels of His love to the ends of the earth. To Him be the glory.

"Listen to me, you who pursue righteousness
and who seek the LORD:
Look to the rock from which you were cut
and to the quarry from which you were hewn;
look to Abraham, your father,
and to Sarah, who gave you birth.
When I called him he was but one,
and I blessed him and made him many."
(Isaiah 51:1–2, NIV)

—Mike Treneer
International President
The Navigators

Acknowledgments

FIRST AND FOREMOST, I THANK Dawson Media editor Leura Jones for her journalistic professionalism in arranging the contents of this book and editing it. Although she is the busy mother of young children, she tackled this project with dedication, understanding, and enthusiasm. The book would not have come into existence without her long hours of hard work and expertise.

My thanks also to Donald McGilchrist, who encouraged me from the beginning and made valuable archived material available for me to refresh my 94-year-old memory.

NavPress editor Don Simpson read my rough notes, and his urging me to pursue the project was most helpful.

Dave Kassing of The Navigators' Development Department deserves much credit for backing this project, for which I express my thanks and gratitude.

Last but not least, thanks and appreciation go to my great wife, Morena, who became a part-time word-processing widow as I spent many hours recapturing memories and transferring them to a computer screen.

Introduction

IN 2006, AN ESTIMATED 6 MILLION people were impacted for Christ through personal contacts and/or publications of The Navigators. These are spiritual descendants of the two men the Lord used to launch and guide The Navigators through its first 53 years. The two men were founder Dawson Trotman and his understudy and successor, Lorne Sanny. As I served alongside them, I had a close-up look into the lives and ministries of these two Navigator legends.

Many of my experiences and observations during that period are known only to me. Lest they go down to the grave with me, I feel compelled to share them with present and future staff of The Navigators, as well as Navigator family and friends. The memories, observations, reflections, and conclusions shared here are my own and may not represent the views of other admirers of these two great men or of the Navigator organization. I welcome feedback from any readers whose knowledge and memory are different from mine so we can make corrections for future editions.

I had a close and unique relationship with Dawson and Lorne, as evidenced in two previous books about Dawson Trotman. Bob Foster, in his book *The Navigator,* wrote, "One of the men closest to Dawson throughout his entire adult life was Jim Downing."

In her book *DAWS,* Betty Skinner wrote, "Dawson came to regard Jim as his deputy in the work and his stand-in for weekend meetings when he was away. . . . Downing was the de facto leader in the fleet."

I joined the Navy in 1932 at the age of 19. During those years of the Great Depression, the Navy was one of the few ways to earn a reliable paycheck and see the world. I was assigned to the Pacific Fleet aboard the USS *West Virginia,* which would later be known as a "floating seminary" because of the impact of the early

Navigators. I met Dawson Trotman while in port in the winter of 1933 and began a friendship with him that would last until his death 23 years later.

My first significant encounter with Lorne Sanny would come in June 1956 when Dawson drowned at Schroon Lake. Shortly after that, I retired from the Navy and moved my family to Colorado Springs to serve as Lorne's assistant as he took the reins as president of The Navigators. Lorne described my role this way in the July 29, 1977, Dear Staff letter: "Jim is my deputy and stands in for me when I am away from the office. His longtime Nav background and comprehension of current thinking, combined with an understanding spirit, ideally fit him to handle many personnel, financial, and public relations matters on my behalf." I would serve with him in that position for the next 22 years.

I was seven years younger than Dawson and seven years older than Lorne. This small age difference allowed me to have a deep friendship with both men. Both had a distinctly human side, as evidenced by their love and care for their families and a willingness to lay down their lives for their friends, should that have been necessary.

Dawson's vision, "don't-say-it-can't-be-done" attitude, and his firm conviction about the promises of God were extensions of his personality. They covered those of us around him like an invisible cloud. My life's ambition was changed when I became his spiritual descendant. I had planned to attend law school and enter political office. After meeting Dawson, my life became all about *availability* to his Lord and mine.

My thankfulness for Lorne Sanny, whom I regarded as my best friend, was best expressed in the prayer I offered to God at Lorne's retirement ceremony in 1986: "We thank you for Lorne's 30 years of fruitful, successful, and inspiring leadership. We thank you for Lorne's example as a man of God and for being a model as one who has challenged us in teaching, way of life, purpose, faith, patience, love, and endurance as he has been a father and pastor to us." (The full prayer is printed in the Appendix of this book.)

It was my privilege to serve at the right hand of these two great men, and here I share some of their stories with you.

PART I

Dawson Trotman

INTRODUCTION

DAWSON TROTMAN WAS DRIVEN by his obsession to see the Great Commission fulfilled. He reasoned that because God commanded that the Good News of Jesus Christ be made known to every person, then it was possible for that imperative to be accomplished.

He once asked me, "If it were possible for you to exchange your salvation for one million dollars, would you do it?"

"No way," I answered.

He said, "God is no respecter of persons. He wants every person on earth to feel the same way as you do about Christ."

Dawson firmly believed that the One who gave the Great Commission had a plan for it to be accomplished. The reason it had not been accomplished in 2,000 years, Dawson reasoned, was that His plan had not been discovered and followed. Dawson's spiritual insight, logical reasoning, and Holy Spirit's prompting helped him conclude that the world would be populated spiritually the same way it is populated physically. Healthy, mature believers should reproduce themselves spiritually in others.

Speaking at Dawson's memorial service in 1956, Billy Graham said that Dawson Trotman had personally impacted more people for Christ than anyone he knew. He said Dawson was always thinking up new schemes to bring people to Christ.

Behind and beyond his schemes was the obsession to bring Christians to maturity, knowing that maturity was the key to reproduction, which was the key to accomplishing the Great Commission.

Meeting the Trotmans

THE YEAR WAS 1933. The month was December. Several of my shipmates aboard the battleship USS *West Virginia*—home ported in San Pedro, California—had told me about a wonderful couple, 27-year-old Dawson Trotman and his 22-year-old wife, Lila.

I was not a Christian, but my shipmate Virgil Hook was. He was "number five" in the small band of men in whose lives Dawson Trotman was having a revolutionary ministry. Virgil prevailed upon me to go ashore with him on a Wednesday afternoon to meet the Trotmans. We were to enjoy some recreation and a home-cooked chicken dinner. Virgil and I took the ship's motor launch to the San Pedro 22nd Street Navy landing and caught a city bus to the stop nearest their apartment. Another shipmate, Lester Spencer, had gone ashore earlier and was on hand to greet us.[1]

From the buildup my friends had given me about Dawson, I expected to see a rugged "superman" type. Instead, I was introduced to a 120-pound man with a small waist, slender ankles, and a head that seemed large in proportion to his body. His heavy beard made him look like he needed a shave a few minutes after applying the razor to his slim, elongated face. Dawson grasped my hand with as firm a grip as his slender arm and bony hand could muster. His voice was of higher pitch than most of the men I had been associating with during my 15 months in the Navy, of which the last 9 had been aboard ship. The fact that he was a civilian—and not too impressive of one at that—was one strike against him in my book.

---

1 Lester Spencer's first-person account of his first interactions with Dawson Trotman is available at www.discipleshiplibrary.com. Look for my name under "Speakers," then scroll to the second page and click on "West Virginia Gang."

Lila was four months younger than I was, though she seemed older. She was noticeably pregnant with their first son Bruce, who would be born a few weeks later. Dawson's Christian associates thought it was worldly to smoke, drink, chew tobacco, dance, or go to the movies, and women's use of cosmetics fell in that same category. Lila went without this modern-day enhancement but was still beautiful, motherly, and hospitable. She impressed me as a perfect wife and hostess.

Both Virgil and Lester were anxious to have Dawson start carving on me with the Sword of the Spirit. During the first lull in our sports activities, I found myself sitting alone with Dawson and an open Bible.

I was deeply impressed that Dawson was sincerely interested in my eternal welfare and was very familiar with the Bible. However, my heart had not been sufficiently plowed for the seed to take root. The only thing I remember from the conversation was that he used the word "iniquities." That word was not part of my vocabulary. Looking back, I think he was explaining Isaiah 53:6 to me: "The LORD hath laid on him the iniquity of us all."

After a delicious dinner, it was time for a meeting. Some other sailors joined us. Dawson began leading us in some Christian choruses, none of which was familiar to me. Singing Christian songs was pretty low on my list of pleasures. I felt trapped. It was too far to walk back to the Navy landing, and I was not experienced enough in the ways of the world to call a taxi.

After a few rafter-shaking songs, there was a knock on the door. The couple from the apartment below asked us to knock off the noise or they would call the police. Dawson chose to exercise his First Amendment right, and the singing continued. Then there came another knock on the door; this time it was two burly policemen. They sternly told us of the complaint, advising us that if there were any further disturbance, we would all be arrested.

I was proud of my impeccable conduct record in the Navy and resented the possibility of it being compromised by a trip to jail. I also resented my well-meaning Christian friends.

The singing stopped, and Dawson probably brought a message from the Word. I don't remember because I was so preoccupied with getting out of there. I tuned him out completely.

The Trotmans' apartment had a couch and some cushions for overnight guests, and they asked me to spend the night with them. I firmly refused and insisted I be taken back to the Navy landing. My shipmates reminded me that the last boat back to the ship left the landing at 10 o'clock, and I had missed it. Still, I prevailed and was driven back to the landing. I spent the night on a hard wooden bench getting very little sleep, but I was happy to have escaped that spiritual prison house.

It took several months to recover from my initial experience in the Trotmans' home. In the meantime, they had moved from San Pedro to an address in Long Beach, soon memorized by scores of men, 33 Surfline.

Several months later, one of the Christians pressured me to go over to the Trotmans' home for a daytime meeting. The new home was within walking distance of the Navy landing, so I knew I had that escape hatch if I chose to use it. The meeting was built around a guest speaker, Oscar Zimmerman, who had a ministry to merchant seamen. His text was 2 Corinthians 9:8, "And God is able to make all grace abound toward you; that ye, always having all sufficiency in all things, may abound to every good work." (That was the translation authorized by King James in 1616. It would be another 25 years before the plethora of translations now available would start to emerge.)

By this time, the Trotmans' son Bruce was crawling. During the message, he pulled himself up to a window sill, retrieved an object, and put it in his mouth. The object filled his little mouth, and he began to discharge noticeable amounts of saliva. One of the sailors picked him up and handed him to Dawson, who reached into Bruce's mouth and retrieved a double-edged razor blade. There was not even a trace of blood in Bruce's mouth. The speaker paused during the procedure. Dawson stood up and said, "Let's thank the Lord for protecting Bruce." He then led in prayer and turned the meeting back over to Mr. Zimmerman.

As I headed back to the ship, I got a message loud and clear. *God was in that home and had a special interest in the family He had commissioned to occupy it for Him.* I knew I had been standing on holy ground.

Shortly thereafter, the USS *West Virginia* left Long Beach to be overhauled at the Bremerton, Washington, naval shipyard. It would be a year before I again crossed paths with the Trotmans. When I did, I would be a different man.

Through the combined influence of the five shipmates of mine whom Dawson had trained, I gave my life to Christ in April 1935. A few days later, numbers three and four of the foundational men Trotman discipled, Dedrick and Goodrick, met with me for follow-up. They began by giving me the Navigator Wheel Illustration, which I bought hook, line, and sinker.

As they explained it to me, a non-Christian sailor who worked with me became curious, and Dedrick turned his attention from me to explain the Gospel to him. I was amazed at the skill and familiarity with which Dedrick used Scripture to answer the man's every question and objection. After seeing that, I learned there was a Scripture memory course published by Moody Bible Institute with about 108 verses to use in personal evangelism. (This was before the days of The Navigators' *Topical Memory System*.) I got a list of the verses and tried prioritizing them by category to help me decide which to memorize first. Because they all seemed of equal importance, I memorized 10 verses a day until I learned them all.

Within a short time, all but one of Dawson's original five band of men, Ed Goodrick, had been discharged from the Navy. The mantle of leadership passed to me, a three-month-old Christian. (Goodrick explains how this came about in LaVerne Tift's book *Valiant in Fight,* page 44.) When I again met Dawson, later in 1935, I had not been appointed officially as the leader but had responsibility for the ship's ministry by default.

The shore ministry was built around a weekly Friday-night meeting in the Trotman living room and a Saturday recreational afternoon followed by another meeting that night. About 18 to 25 people attended, most of them new Christians brought to the home by more mature believers. After a round of fun and singing, Dawson would speak. His presentations were lengthy, sometimes lasting nearly two hours. If attention waned, he sometimes carried a cap pistol in his back pocket that he would fire to shock away the drowsiness.

Because half of the ship's crew was required to be aboard at all times, the Friday and Saturday night groups consisted of different sailors. I had a special position aboard ship so I was free both Friday and Saturday nights.

One day Dawson said to me, "Jim, I really appreciate you sitting through all of those long meetings and being attentive, even though there is a lot of repetition."

I responded by telling him I generally had someone with me who was profiting from the meetings. Then I added, "I do have a suggestion. I think if you would take more time in preparing, it wouldn't take so long to give your message."

His reply was instant: "I see you don't understand."

"Apparently I do not," I said. "What is it I don't understand?"

He rose to his full height, stretched out his square jaw for emphasis, and thundered as much as his high-pitched voice would allow, "I am determined that no person in that room will ever be the same after that meeting. *That takes a little more time.*"

This admonition sharpened my powers of observation, and I began to catch on.

After a relaxed introduction, he would select one of the elements of the Wheel Illustration to speak on, Scripture memory for example. He would make a convincing argument for memorizing Scripture, during which he would make eye contact with every one of his listeners. He could tell by their body language where they stood regarding Scripture memory. Some would look him in the eye and beam and nod approval. Others would look away and avoid his piercing eyes. He would then zero in on this crowd and multiply the reasons for memorizing. He would continue this barrage until several had raised their heads in resolve, silently acknowledging, "You have convinced me. I am ready to start memorizing."

The Wheel Illustration may well be Dawson's most lasting legacy.

He would then take another subject, such as witnessing, prayer, or Bible study, and repeat the process until he had uncovered a deficit in the life of everyone present and preached them into making a change. That did indeed take a little time, and we in the fleet appreciated having him motivate some of the men we were working with more effectively than we could.

When I understood his strategy, it energized my mean streak. I would often sit in the meeting absolutely expressionless. When he zeroed in on me but got no response, he would call me by name and ask how I was doing in the area he was emphasizing. After a few such incidents, we had a talk. I knew the areas in which he was struggling. I told him that the next time he called on me by name in a meeting, I was going to respond by asking him how he was doing in the areas he struggled in. A truce followed.

Throughout my time in the Navy, Dawson asked me to be a Navigator representative in the area in which we were located. When we moved to Honolulu in 1952, I asked him for an update on what I was expected to do.

"You know what to do," he replied.

When I insisted that he verbalize his expectations, he raised his voice and said, somewhat impatiently, "Do what you have always done. *Lead people to Christ and build them up to where they can repeat the process.*"

The ministry of The Navigators never got more complicated to him than that. He had observed that in every culture he knew of, when Christ-centered Christians started memorizing Scripture, praying, studying the Bible, and witnessing, spiritual revolution was obvious.

8

The First Nav Home

WHEN THE TROTMANS FIRST BEGAN ministering to a handful of sailors, their home was a garage-like structure behind the gas station where Dawson was employed. He often compared his ministry to filling cars with gasoline so they could get on their way and accomplish their task. He said his role was not doing ministry on the warships like the sailors did, but getting the men spiritually refueled to get on with their mission.

When the Trotmans moved from San Pedro—where I first met them—to Long Beach in 1934, they rented a cottage-like home on the waterfront within walking distance of the Navy landing. The house at 33 Surfline adjoined a huge, noisy amusement park known as The Pike. Many of the fleet's single men went there for recreation.

The home was not in the most wholesome neighborhood. Living in one of the nearby apartments were some women whose occupation was unknown. They would sometimes parade around the room in the nude, and if they perceived someone was watching, they would throw back the curtain and stand in front of the window. Dawson practiced as well as preached 1 Corinthians 10:13 and was not tempted to be unfaithful. Still, he was so sensitive to sin that he once told me, "I forfeited my right to lead The Navigators." He was referring to the fact that he may have allowed his eyes to linger momentarily rather than flee immediately.

This experience left the lifelong impression on his heart and mind that The Navigators was a work of God and was not dependent on his performance. This realization was reinforced by Dawson's lack of robust physique.

One afternoon, Dawson, Elroy Robinson, and I were resting on the side of a swimming pool after some strenuous competition. Elroy was an internationally known, world-class distance runner from Fresno State. Dawson looked at Elroy, whose leg and chest muscles never seemed to relax but rippled with uncontrolled energy—even when he was lying still.

Dawson looked at his own skinny legs and mused: "I used to have a quarrel with God because He made me so slight. But I reasoned that if God ever used me in a significant way, people might attribute it to my having an Atlas-like physique. But if He used this skinny guy, God—not man—would get the glory."

Elroy was quick on the mental trigger. "How do you think that makes me feel?"

Except for his muscles, Elroy was not the most handsome man on the block.

Without a microsecond delay, Dawson responded, "Elroy, as ugly as you are, you have a greater disadvantage than I will ever have."

The Trotmans' second home in Long Beach was on one of the main streets a mile from downtown. The rented house was located at 1114 Pacific Avenue. It was while they lived there that Ruth was born. During that time, Lila was unable to do the cooking, so Dawson took over. He did everything with excellence and style. He donned a white apron and chef's cap while in the kitchen. One day, one of the men, who happened to be a lightweight boxer in the fleet, arrived while Dawson was dressed in his kitchen regalia.

When the sailor called Dawson a sissy, Dawson grabbed a skillet and chased him out into the yard and in several circles around the house. The only thing that saved the young man from a bump on the head was that he outran Dawson.

Dawson traveled extensively during those years. When our ship went to sea for gunnery practice, I stayed behind to have the mail ready when the ship came back into port. I stayed at the Trotman home, and in Dawson's absence, I became the "man of the house" as well as tending to the ministry. I had many pleasant hours babysitting Ruth. When she began to talk, she called me "Din Din."

I did not realize the intense scrutiny I was under until one day Dawson commended me for being a perfect gentleman while he was away. Lila was monitoring me very diligently.

But I did get into deep trouble once.

At that time, many Sunday schools used the same lessons. They were called the International Sunday School lessons. An editor by the name of Trumball published a 16-or-so-page periodical called the *Sunday School Times*. It gave every possible explanation, interpretation, and application of the Scripture that would be used in that Sunday's lesson. It also contained a weekly cartoon by master artist E.J. Pace illustrating the lesson. But most used was a page of great illustrations covering almost every verse in the lesson.

While Dawson was away one time, I used one of these illustrations in a presentation. By stretching the imagination, the illustration could be interpreted in more than one way. Lila interpreted it as an off-color joke. My credibility was gone. When Dawson confronted me, he was ready to drum me out of the Navigator corps. It was only when I showed him a printed copy of the illustration in the highly respected *Sunday School Times* that I was restored.

The Trotmans' next big step of faith was to purchase a home five miles from downtown Long Beach at 4845 East 6th Street. A Coast Guard officer provided most of the $3,000 to pay for the house. (In 2000, Navigator staff Randy Weyeneth, checking on historical sites, photographed the home, which had a for-sale sign in front. The asking price was $435,000.)

It was a small house but an ideal choice for the booming years of the fleet ministry. It was only a hundred yards from a well-equipped city park and was only a few blocks from the end of the bus line. There was room outside for sports, including our favorite, volleyball. Nearby was a golf course and an all-weather pavilion for cookouts, as well as a lagoon that became our Jordan River for baptisms. (Trotman followed what he believed was the baptismal style practiced by the first-century Christians, triune baptism. The person was placed in a fetal position and immersed three times, in the name of the Father, the Son, and the Holy Spirit.)

The Trotman home became a model for the emerging military ministry. In a few years, Navigator homes popped up near many military bases. The home atmosphere filled an inner heart vacuum for young men away from home. One of the first four

Navigators, Ed Goodrick, told Dawson that he thought he was coming to the house to hear some great teaching. What he realized, he said, was that "the men put up with Dawson just to be around Lila and the home."

Creator, Inventor, Counselor

PRACTICING THE BASICS of the Wheel Illustration in his own life was as natural and habitual for Dawson as eating and breathing. But this was not true of all those with whom he teamed up. His perfectionist nature and achiever's drive kept him always striving for a way to help people do better. His creative mind was always conjuring up new tools—pages for memory verses, reviewed verses, prayer pages, and Bible studies. He gradually added address pages and many of the items in today's day-planner books. These had the collective name of "Daily Check Up," commonly known as DCU.

Some of his ideas may not have been 100 percent original. Dawson was a friend of a radio pastor named Milo Jameson, who had a daily broadcast over one of the most powerful radio stations in Southern California. He provided his listeners with devotional studies and a tract-like folder with blocks to check to show faithfulness and progress in Bible reading, prayer, and so forth. Several of us in the fleet used these helps.

Dawson packaged some of his tools in a notebook and met with Milo Jameson to share his innovation. I saw Dawson just after this meeting. He was noticeably deflated and upset. Instead of commending him, Milo had said, "Dawson, you have stolen everything I have." Milo apparently thought Dawson had taken his ideas and expanded and refined them. Fortunately, this did not jeopardize their friendship.

The sheets for these notebooks were first typed or handprinted on a mimeograph stencil. Dawson's clever artwork was added and then reproduced on different-colored paper on a mimeograph machine. The paper had to be porous to absorb the ink. The life of a mimeograph stencil is only a few dozen copies. The black ink was prone to smear, making it a messy operation.

Soon Dawson was able to get enough money together ($15) to purchase a used printing press. It had a treadle and was driven like a bicycle. Sheets of paper were fed one by one onto a big circular disk, and a big black roller covered with black ink reproduced material from a master sheet to the blank paper. Operating it was sort of like rubbing your head and patting your stomach at the same time. Sometimes one of us sailors was recruited to feed the paper while Dawson pedaled.

Every Navigator sailor carried a 5x7-inch black looseleaf notebook filled with colored pages. (Later, when some of our men visited overseas missionaries, they wrote to Dawson asking for notebooks. They had concluded that the secret of the sailors' spiritual vitality was the notebook.)

Dawson knew sailors spent a lot of time waiting in line for meals, paychecks, and the like, and he encouraged them to use this time to memorize and review their verses. But they countered, "A sailor's uniform doesn't have any pockets to carry a New Testament or even a Gospel of John." (It was the view of the naval decision-makers that if a sailor had pants pockets he would put his hands in them and that would be detrimental to military posture.) The only pocket in a sailor's uniform is a breast pocket on the left side of the pullover part of his uniform.

Dawson and his close friend Lewie Coates had created their own program of Scripture memory, using blank cards to write out their memory verses. They then filed them by topics in boxes.

One day when I arrived at the Trotman home, I saw a sailor in Dawson's office with his jumper removed. Dawson had it laid out on his desk and was measuring the size of the pocket.

He then cut up some cards that fit the pocket. The sailors could write verses on these cards and memorize and review Scripture while waiting in line or otherwise passing time. Dawson was not a fan of printed verse cards. He felt that writing them out in one's own handwriting was a huge start in the memorizing process.

Dawson decided there should be guidelines for prioritizing the memory verses rather than each sailor selecting his own. As he worked on this one afternoon, I witnessed the birth of the *Topical Memory System,* known to people around the world as the TMS. Dawson and Coates were sitting at a table with their verses filed in boxes by topic. They selected a group of topics and decided the number of verses to be memorized on each topic. Occasionally, some heated exchanges occurred as they selected the verses, each insisting his verses were the best for the topic. I couldn't have imagined the blessing to the world that would result from this not-too-spiritual-appearing exercise. But apparently the Lord prevailed, and the verses best suited were chosen. Soon a printed list of memory verses was distributed to Navigators.

(I have sometimes second-guessed this structured approach to Scripture memory. In my own experience, there are certain verses I can't forget and certain ones I can't remember. Perhaps a more balanced approach would be to memorize both from a structured list and from one we create ourselves with verses we feel we just have to memorize. When the first generation of Navigators sat around the table sharing memorized verses, there was always notetaking to write down and memorize the verses that had helped another in a particular situation.)

Although tools were important to Dawson, he never lost sight of the preeminence of God's Word. After getting to know Dawson, I asked him what I needed to be fully equipped as a functioning Christian. He helped me get a *Scofield Reference Bible, Cruden's Concordance, Smith's Bible Dictionary, Torrey's Topical Textbook,* and Evans's *Great Doctrines of the Bible.* Along with the notebook, these five books became standard equipment for those who wanted to get down to business. Although a bit cumbersome to tuck under the arm, they constituted the entire library Dawson believed we needed.

His rationale was demonstrated by the following incident. We were discussing the Holy Spirit and the matter of being baptized by the Spirit and exercising or not exercising charismatic gifts. Dawson said that after he became a Christian, his mother was delighted. She belonged to a charismatic group and tried to persuade him that to be a complete Christian, he needed to be baptized with the Holy Spirit and speak in tongues. Dawson had some questions about this.

So he took his Bible and concordance and went up into the hills for a few days. He looked up and studied every verse in the Bible that mentioned the Holy Spirit.

Wide-eyed, I asked, "What did you conclude?"

Without batting an eye he said, "You have the same Bible as I do. Find out for yourself."

He never again commented on his belief about the matters I had inquired about.

He expected us to learn the Bible by digging into it rather than listening to others talk about it. One of his cartoons in the mimeograph days was a donkey and prospector equipped with pick and shovel who had just uncovered a large nugget of gold, illustrating verses like Psalm 119:127: "I love thy commandments above gold; yea, above fine gold."

Counselor

My first counseling session with Dawson came as a result of my deep concern over my failure to discern and follow what I thought was the will of God. There were no structured Sunday plans during those early days of The Navigators. We were free to attend any church we wanted. I personally liked to visit the well-known conservative evangelical churches in the Los Angeles area. In my Sunday-morning quiet time, I would map out a routine for the day, assume God had guided me in it, and then proceed. One Sunday morning I attended a large church service. I didn't speak to anyone, and no one spoke to me. In that incident and several others that day, I could not see any evidence that the Lord had led or had anything special in mind. My conclusion: Because I couldn't discern the Lord's will, it seemed like the Christian life was futile. I was about to become a major backslider.

Very troubled, I counseled with Dawson at 33 Surfline. After hearing my story and asking a few questions, he told me, "When you kneel down before the Lord, no matter how spiritual you are or think you are, it is still about 90 percent you and 10 percent God."

I could see how I had been planning my own routine, not always based on a word from God. That was the beginning of a more step-by-step, little-by-little process of following the Lord, rather than asking for a detailed battle plan in advance that produced the results I expected.

Counseling is a vital part of the spiritual nurturing of a new and growing Christian. Today, we have an abundance of resources to help us counsel others. Dawson probably never attended a seminar on the fine art of spiritual counseling. Consequently, he never mastered the practice of "indirect counseling"—helping others discover, select, and choose the best available option. Dawson's counseling was mostly verses of Scripture, and being a man of practical wisdom, he generally had a solution for every problem.

Building Generations

IN THOSE EARLY DAYS IN THE MID-1930s as I got better acquainted with Dawson, he invited me periodically to spend the day with him and accompany him on his appointments. On one of my days off, he picked me up at the Navy landing. Instead of taking me to his home, he pulled the car into the nearest parking place. Sitting behind the wheel of the 1932 Packard, he opened his King James Bible to Isaiah 58. He said excitedly, "I have something I have to show you." He put the Bible in front of me and read verse 12:

"And they that shall be of thee shall build the old waste places: thou shalt raise up the foundations of many generations; and thou shalt be called, The repairer of the breach, The restorer of paths to dwell in."

He confided, "I am scared to death, but I know God has told me He is going to do this through me."

As Dawson read that verse to me with such assurance, I resolved that I would throw my life in with him. I realized he was involved in the major leagues of life both here and hereafter, and I wanted to be included.

In the years that followed, Lorne Sanny often asked in our leadership team meetings, "What promise has God given you lately?"

While the others shared freely, I was embarrassed. I had no new verse.

That experience with Trotman had given me Isaiah 58:12 for a lifetime. Since then it has been supplemented by many of the other estimated 7,487 promises in the Bible, but to me, Isaiah 58:12 is *"the promise."*

With such a promise burning in Dawson's soul, he was naturally anxious to get on with fulfilling it. The work with the fleet was only a part-time job due to the nature of the Navy and its demands. Saturday afternoons and evenings were the big thrust when the fleet was in port. There were also the Friday-night meetings, and some of the men came over on Wednesday afternoons.

The fleet spent at least half of the time at sea in training maneuvers. Every summer, we had cruises to Hawaii and to Seattle and Tacoma. In the 1930s, we had two cruises to New York and other East Coast cities that lasted for months. We were without Dawson's leadership during those times and had to provide our own.

In 1939, about a third of the fleet, normally based at Long Beach, was split off to form the Hawaiian Detachment home ported at Pearl Harbor. Dawson recruited his seminary classmate Harold DeGroff and his wife, Belva, to move to Honolulu and establish a Navigator home. The ministry modeled in Long Beach continued in Honolulu. The residence at 2744 Kalihi Street was built on stone piling about six feet above ground. This huge crawl space, with a floor made of wood chips, was our auditorium. The Saturday-night meetings drew as many as 120. On Sundays, the porch and yard were filled as we gathered around the radio to listen to Charles Fuller on his *Old Fashioned Revival Hour* broadcast. During the next nine years, more than 25,000 servicemen visited this home.

In 1940, the remainder of the Pacific Fleet changed its home base from Long Beach to Pearl Harbor. With the lack of fleet activity in Long Beach, Dawson moved to a new location at 175 Virgil Street in Hollywood. He established his office in the Willard Hotel in downtown Los Angeles, adjacent to the Bible Institute of Los Angeles (BIOLA) and the Church of the Open Door. These two institutions were strongholds of conservative evangelical Christianity in Southern California.

Although Dawson visited Honolulu a couple of times, his main interest reverted to high school boys and girls Bible clubs, which he called Dunamis and Martures, respectively. Lorne Sanny and my future wife, Morena, were both recruited as BIOLA students to help with these clubs.

The foundation of Isaiah 58:12, however, was laid among military men. God foresaw what man couldn't have seen: The Navy ship, particularly the battleship, was a perfect laboratory for what God wanted to do. Christians had unique opportunities and motivation aboard these ships.

About 1,500 officers and crew were required to operate a battleship. While at sea, the crew had no access to newspapers or radio. There were few books and of course no satellites, computers, TVs, or DVDs. When we sailed over the horizon, it was as though we entered a black hole as far as the rest of the universe was concerned. We had no distractions.

The workday ended at 3:30 P.M., followed by two hours for leisure and taking care of personal necessities like laundry. The evening meal was finished by 6:00. Those men not on watch had an hour-and-a-half window of free time until the movie was shown on the fantail of the ship, weather and training maneuvers permitting.

With men idle everywhere, those 90 minutes were prime time for evangelism. The Christians fanned out throughout the ship connecting with those we had prayed for and making new contacts.

Aboard the *West Virginia,* we met for team prayer three times a day. Nearly everyone on the ship not on watch attended the movie, so we had an additional two and a half hours to meet together every evening. Attendance was not mandatory because evangelism, personal development, and one-on-one time with the newer Christians were higher priorities. As the number of new Christians grew, one team would take responsibility for them and duplicate what the core team was doing.

Our weekly evangelism study was announced over the ship's loudspeaker so everyone onboard was aware of it. For the Christians to attend, they had to bring at least one non-Christian or prove they had spent at least one hour trying to get someone to come. Failure to do so subjected them to spiritual probation.

Our evening routine looked like this:

Monday 7:30 to 10:00—New Testament chapter study
Tuesday 7:30 to 8:30—Evangelistic Bible study for the
    ship's crew
Wednesday 7:30 to 10:00—Prayer study and extended
    prayer meeting

Thursday 7:30 to 10:00—Old Testament chapter study
Friday 7:30 to 10:00—Biblical topic study

Saturday afternoons were prime times for evangelism, and we attended the ship's Sunday-morning worship service at sea. There were few evangelical chaplains in the Navy. The content of most sermons was "lift yourself up by your own bootstraps." We were instructed that if we did something nice, saw something nice, and said something nice every day, we would be right with God and man.

We had a mini-conference on Sunday afternoons. We carried a library of sermons by Spurgeon, Moody, Torrey, and other great preachers and took turns reading them as a substitute for having a speaker. (Tape recording had not yet been invented.)

One of the strengths of the battleship setup was that every new Christian had a role model. When a sailor decided to follow Christ, he followed in the steps of his spiritual father and knew what to do. He received instruction from someone he knew and trusted. It was as John Dewey said: "Example is not the best method of teaching; *it is the only way.*"

CHAPTER 5

Expanding Generations

DAWSON TROTMAN LIVED TO SEE the *foundation* of many generations but not the waves of generations that would follow. The second half of the 20th century would see the most dramatic growth of Christian faith and practice since the early centuries after Christ's time on earth.

During the 39 years between 1950 and 1989, the population of the world doubled. During this same period, the number of people on earth who call themselves Christians more than doubled, increasing from 854 million to 1.7 billion. The number of Christians who meet the profile of a disciple, which missiologists call "Great Commission Christians," grew from 80 million to 500 million, an amazing increase of 525 percent during those 39 years.[1]

At the close of World War II, the number of Christian missionaries serving overseas increased rapidly, growing from about 18,000 to more than 150,000 today.

What accounted for this encouraging burst of outreach?

According to missionary author Roy Robertson, the fourth and most recent significant advance in world missions grew out of the ministry of men and women impacted by God while serving in the military before and during World War II. One researcher estimates that 25,000 new laborers for Christ emerged from World War II.

The Navigators were vitally involved in fueling this movement. The first wave of Navigator generations was in the Navy. As an incentive to reenlist, the government gave a sailor the opportunity to choose any ship in the Navy for his next assignment. This was

---

1 Statistics from *Perspectives on the World Christian Movement*; published by the William Carey Library.

a perfect provision for us. We prayed over a list of ships on which we wanted to send out team members. Several alumni of the *West Virginia* "floating seminary" received a Navy missionary assignment to another ship.

Multiplication was going on all around us. While docked, Christian sailors brought their non-Christian friends to more than a dozen Navigator homes and Servicemen's Centers manned by Navigator staff. Dawson Trotman stated that men from every one of the then 48 states had come to Christ in his living room.

Dawson made an invitational speaking tour to a few Bible schools and Christian colleges shortly after the war ended. He reported that at least 400 students in these schools said they had come out of the Navigator military ministry.

At the conclusion of World War II, Dawson urged those impacted by the Navigator ministry to go overseas. The first two issues of the *Navigators Log* after the war were devoted to listing names and addresses of overseas mission organizations and providing help in how to apply to these missions. Soon Navigators were accepted by and serving with more than 40 mission agencies.

Wycliffe Bible Translators was a favorite choice for new missionary candidates. Once while speaking in a public meeting, Wycliffe director Cameron Townsend spotted Dawson Trotman and a few sailors in the audience. Pointing him out, Townsend said, "Dawson, I want 500 men from The Navigators ministry to join Wycliffe."

There was a long pause. Dawson responded, "If it is the Lord's will, we will provide them." Townsend quickly replied, "It is the Lord's will. You get 'em."

A Focus on Follow-Up

The passage of Scripture I heard Dawson preach on more than any other was Colossians 1:28. His King James Bible put it this way:

"Whom we preach, warning every man, and teaching every man in all wisdom; that we may present every man *perfect* in Christ Jesus."

The footnote in Dawson's Bible cross-referenced Matthew 5:48, which explained that the word *perfect* means "to be fully mature."

This is what The Navigators was about—follow-up, man-to-man, generations, multiplication, reproducing. They all overlapped.

One weekend Dawson took three of us for a "think-tank" weekend in the mountains near San Bernardino, California. He was wrestling with the idea of follow-up, wondering why Christians who get off to a seemingly good start often fall by the wayside. Actually, he did most of the thinking that weekend. Our main contribution was being a sounding board. He concluded that if a new Christian did not mature, it was due to a lack of follow-up.

At the conclusion of our time together, he pronounced to us: "You have no right to lead someone to Christ unless you are going to follow them up." Later he would say, "You have no right to leave your orphan on someone else's doorstep."

I countered with the idea that we really don't decide who is coming to Christ. If the Holy Spirit is prompting us to help someone come to Christ, we had better obey. After all, the new Christian would have the benefits of the indwelling of the Holy Spirit and the Bible. But Dawson didn't budge from his position.

I decided to try the mother of all follow-up tests in my own "laboratory" involving a man named Glen I had recently led to Christ. I met with him for quiet time every morning. In the 10 A.M. morning mail, I sent him a verse of Scripture. I met with him at noon for Bible study and Scripture memory. In the afternoon mail, I sent him another verse of Scripture. I met with him again in the evening. I took him with me to meetings and accompanied him on his errands and recreation ashore. If he went ashore alone, I waited up so we could pray together before turning in.

Perhaps I mothered him to death. Gradually, he started missing meetings and began avoiding me more and more. We remained friends and he called on me to help him in his courtship and to secure a marriage license. But he just didn't grow spiritually. This experience helped me conclude that lack of follow-up isn't the only factor that keeps a Christian from reaching maturity.

Later I was helped by Dr. Walter Lewis Wilson, who was one of our favorite speakers at Navigator events. I asked him why it was that two new Christians who had identical follow-up would turn out so differently. One would take off like a rocket in his spiritual life, while another seemed to be dragging an anchor.

Dr. Wilson answered by telling me I wasn't the first to be burdened by this problem. It had been the burden of Christian workers since the beginning of Christianity.

He then took me to the parable of the sower in the New Testament. His analysis was that of the seed that fell on the good ground, some would produce thirtyfold, some sixtyfold, and some hundredfold. He said that if you saw a thirtyfold Christian, 70 percent of the time there was no evidence they were a Christian. He ended by saying, "I don't know why it is this way, but God anticipated that this is the way it would be." He suggested that the hundredfold Christian was more rare than routine.

Perhaps as the farmer is responsible for the condition of the soil on his farm, we are responsible for the condition of our hearts and whether we will produce a thirtyfold, sixtyfold, or hundredfold return for our Landlord.

Spiritual Reproduction

Follow-up was the key to spiritual maturity, Dawson believed, and spiritual maturity was the key to spiritual reproduction. Dawson wrote an article for the *Far Eastern Gospel Crusade* magazine called "Making Your Witness Count." It gave the account of how I had led Kenny Watters to Christ, who in turn had led Don Rosenberger to Christ. To Dawson, at that time, this story illustrated that generations were the alpha and omega of the Christian life. (A copy of this article is in the Appendix of this book.)

Missionary executive Don Hamilton told me about a time he was traveling with Dawson and had a surprising encounter. They crossed paths with one of Don's old friends, who asked, "Don, what are you doing now?" He introduced his friend to Dawson and said, "I am a Navigator."

As they went on their way, Dawson asked Don, "Did I hear you say you were a Navigator?"

"Of course I did," Don replied.

"What makes you think you are a Navigator?"

Don answered, "I'm in your Bible study and on your ministry team. I travel and minister with you."

"You're no Navigator," Dawson told him.

"What makes you say that?" Don asked.

"Where are your spiritual grandchildren?" was Dawson's response.

I encountered this fierce passion myself in New York City. My ship was in the Brooklyn Navy yard in the late 1940s, and Dawson was returning from one of his round-the-world trips. We had arranged to meet at his hotel. He briefed me on his trip and then began to quiz me about my family and ministry. If I recall accurately, he interrupted me six or eight times with the question, "Yes, I understand, but *where's your man?*" He exhorted me more strongly than ever before, as if my answer was unsatisfactory. I left with the impression that he felt any Christian who was not majoring in helping someone else just wasn't with it. At that time, there was only one string on his ministry fiddle: "Where's your man or woman?"

In fact, this became Dawson's most widely known message, eventually published in the booklet *Born to Reproduce*. The content of the booklet was originally a talk he had given to the staff of Back to the Bible. They packaged it in the now-famous booklet.[1]

Dawson did not come up with the title. A more appropriate title would have been *A Passionate Call to Maturity, Spiritual Reproduction, and Spiritual Parenting to Help Fulfill the Great Commission*, but maybe that was too long. The content amplifies principles in Dawson's booklet *Follow Up: Conserving the Fruits of Evangelism*. More than anything, it was a 5,700-word, 47-minute summary of the issues that burned deeply in Dawson Trotman's soul.

The spiritual generations traced back to Dawson Trotman and the early Navigators brought a great deal of growth and maturity to the body of Christ. When the Lord called Dawson and Lila to minister to a few sailors, little did they realize how God would use

---

1 I have developed a half-day seminar using *Born to Reproduce,* available at www.discipleshiplibrary.com.

military men and women to further His mission. Their service for Him was not only the foundation of The Navigators ministry today, but was part of one of the greatest missional leaps forward in all of history.

In the late 1980s, I served as a consultant to Dr. Ralph Winter, then-president of the U.S. Center for World Mission in Pasadena. One day I told a missionary leader there about my background with The Navigators. He remarked, "It is hard to find a missionary leader today whose life has not been significantly impacted by The Navigators."

Exhorter and Perfectionist

THE GREEK WORD FOR "EXHORT" appears 109 times in the New Testament. Twenty-six times it is translated "urge" or "urged to." Dawson clearly had this gift, and it was vigorously reproduced in the early Navigators. Some other Christians who did not appreciate the employment of this gift characterized Navigator men as "thinking they are little Holy Spirits going around convicting everyone else."

In 1953, Dawson came to Honolulu and attended a weekend conference with us. Because he was interested in and active with Youth for Christ (YFC) and was on their board of directors, he asked me if the local director was coming to the conference.

I answered that he had been invited but would not be coming.

"Why isn't he coming?" Dawson asked.

I responded, "Do you really want to know?"

When he said, "Certainly," I told him I had invited the YFC director and then I shared his response. "No thanks," the man had told me. "I spent a week with Dawson Trotman at Camp Bethel, and I got enough of him to last me the rest of my life."

Dawson then told me that the greatest burden he carried was the trail of wounded souls he had left around the world. "Some people think I have the gift of exhortation and enjoy exercising it," he said. "They are wrong. Exhorting others is very difficult for me. I only do it out of sheer obedience lest I ignore and grieve the Holy Spirit."

Some of us on the other end of the exhortations may not have always had the spiritual discernment to realize it was for our own good.

Driven to Perfection

The Navigators purchased Glen Eyrie in 1953 and began to fully occupy the former estate of Colorado Springs founder General William Palmer in 1954. During that first summer, a grass fire broke out on the southeast corner of the property. It had been a dry summer, and there were heavy grass and considerable brush on much of the property. Fanned by the ever-present breezes, the fire spread rapidly and threatened some of the eight buildings on the property. With the help of neighbors, the fire department, and all of the Glen Eyrie crew, the fire was finally extinguished after a strenuous two-hour battle.

As the lead firefighter, Dawson wanted to know what had caused the fire.

A former owner had constructed an outdoor incinerator from five 8x8-foot square panels. They were made by welding squares of expanded metal (heavy iron screens) to concrete reinforcing rods. They were then erected in the form of a square with one panel as the roof. They were wired together so that the south panel could be used as a door.

For 28 years, the property had only been used as a summer home, and the incinerator had fallen into disrepair. The wires holding the panels together had rusted, leaving a sagging roof and large gaps between the panels.

One of the office workers had been told there was an incinerator in which he could burn papers. On this particular day, the wind had caught some of the burning papers, blowing them through one of the gaping holes and starting the fire.

Once the fire was extinguished, Dawson gathered the tired, dirty, sweaty crew around the site. He had a low tolerance for stupidity, and the idea that an intelligent human being would burn papers in what was the equivalent of an open fire in gusty wind really agitated him. He lectured the crew as though each one were individually responsible. As he reflected on the carelessness that had caused the near tragedy, he almost exhausted his vocabulary. After several repetitions, the attention span of some of the weary firefighters began to wane.

Dawson responded, "You think I am a perfectionist. You're right. I am. And furthermore, if I were not a perfectionist, there would not be a Navigator ministry today."

We have all had some interaction with perfectionists. Dawson epitomized the profile. He was driven by the probability that there must be a better way to do everything. Many times a group of us worked late into the night with Dawson to find a solution to a problem. Finally, we went to bed believing the problem's solution had been achieved. Yet we were often shocked to hear first thing in the morning, "There must be a better way." Then we would start all over again.

But there was one problem Dawson laid to rest. The "perfectionist" was content with the conclusion that the world could only be populated spiritually the same way it was populated physically, with every Christian brought to maturity so that they could reproduce themselves spiritually. To this concept, Dawson Trotman gave all his adult life and energy.

Matchmaker

ALTHOUGH THE NAVIGATORS WERE occasionally known as "The Never-Daters," that heritage didn't come from Dawson's genes. When he smelled romance blooming, he followed it through with the persistence of a bloodhound on the trail.

I first crossed paths with Morena Holmes at Dawson's office in Los Angeles. She was one of the Bible Institute of Los Angeles students who led his high school girls (Martures) Bible clubs. She was there to consult with him on Bible club business, and I was there on fleet business.

Morena was a member of BIOLA's mixed quartet. Dawson invited this quartet to sing at the Navigator Saturday-night meetings on several occasions. The members of the quartet gave their testimonies, and I was particularly impressed with Morena's walk with God.

Later, the quartet was invited to attend the nearly all-men's annual Life Triumphant in Christ conference in Pacific Palisades, California. At one of the meals, I saw a vacant chair next to Morena and sat down beside her. Among the hardline fleet Navigators, this caused quite a stir. A rumor began to buzz: "Downing's got a girl."

Because mature Christian sailors were such a rarity, we met a lot of girls our age who wanted help with Scripture memory and other areas of their Christian lives. Many had friends they wanted us to help too. As a result, the guys had a lot of correspondence with the girls. When it looked like it was getting out of hand, we made a rule. The fellows could take down names and addresses and note the particular need. They could refer the girl to an appropriate person but not give out their own names and addresses. Hence, to even sit next to a girl raised eyebrows.

Dawson and Lila detected I had more than a passing interest in Morena. They took special measures to see that I accompanied them to Morena's graduation from BIOLA in June 1940. She was the graduating class women's speaker and really wowed the audience, me included. I had prayed that if the Lord wanted us to get better acquainted, I would have the opportunity to speak to her after the ceremony. Miraculously, the circle of admirers and well wishers around her parted like the Red Sea, and I found her standing alone.

We talked briefly about future ministry. Unknown to the other, we started praying for one another. (One of the fleeces I had out for the right helpmate was that she would pray for me at least six months before I found out about it.)

Morena was to spend the summer with a Child Evangelism Fellowship team in the rural south. Dawson invited her to move into their home in Long Beach when she finished her assignment. After she left for the summer, Dawson handed me a letter he had gotten from Morena and a handwritten note marked "personal." It is still a treasured part of my files.

It said:

"Hi Jim.

"Boy oh boy. I told Morena what I'd told you and that you said that you weren't surprised. Took her off her feet. Upon inquiry she told Lila and I she was thrilled and scared. Enclosed letter came after we had left a small gift just as she left.

"I put Pro. 31:19 'whoso findeth,' hence the comment in letter—ask me about the meaning of the part where the arrow is.

"Personally I regard M.H. as one of the 3 or 4 most outstanding women I have known in the years of my Christian life (some 14). When I told her you were #1 Navigator—boy, she smiled beautiful 'n everything."

Morena moved in with the Trotman family in September of 1940. Because the home was small, she had no separate room but slept on the living-room sofa. She could not turn in for the night until all the guests had left, which was often late.

I was with the fleet cruising in the South Pacific. On one of our trips, we crossed the equator. By tradition, this calls for a special ceremony to initiate all pollywogs into the kingdom of Neptunus Rex. Pollywogs are those who have never crossed the equator. The brutal initiation is done by shellbacks, those who have previously crossed the equator. After the initiation, we had the rest of the day off.

I spent the extra time with the Lord and did some heart searching. As I asked the Lord if there was anything I needed to do to be perfectly right with Him, it seemed as though He asked, "How about Morena?" I couldn't help but think, "That's not what I meant."

But as an act of obedience, a little scared, I wrote her a letter stating my interest in a future together. I didn't mail it.

My ship was stationed in Pearl Harbor, but we made an extended visit to Long Beach in the fall of 1940, lasting past Christmas. I spent my spare time at the Trotman home where Morena was living. One of her jobs was editor of the *Navigators Log*.

One night Dawson and Lila set up a situation designed to speed up a relationship. Dawson and Lila said Morena needed background on the men she would be writing about in the *Navigators Log*. They said that because I knew the men better than anyone else, I should give her a briefing. Dawson had his desk and files in one of the bedrooms. We sat down together in there and began to leaf through some files. Dawson and Lila and the other guests had retired to the living room to plot and pray.

After a few minutes of pretending to carry out our artificial assignment, I saw through this not-too-subtle setup. I suggested to Morena that we join the others in the living room. I shall never forget the surprised looks on their faces as we joined them after such a brief tryst.

The next day, Dawson really got on my case. He said, "Listen, Morena isn't the kind of girl who will wait around. If you don't make a move, someone else will."

I am not proud of my ungrateful response: "If someone else can get her, that is all the proof I need that God doesn't intend her for me."

A few nights later, I needed to make a trip to San Pedro to pick up some Tagalog tracts for a friend who was going to the Philippines. I asked Morena to go with me. She had dishwashing duty that night, but Dawson and Lila moved heaven and earth to find a substitute so she could go with me.

Before I went into the house in San Pedro, I handed her the unmailed letter I had written her months before. Back at Long Beach, we discussed the letter. I had some clarifying to do. She regarded the letter as a marriage proposal, but I had not intended that yet.

The next day, however, as we sat parked overlooking the Pacific, I knew the time had come. The feeling in my heart spilled over into my stomach. I felt uneasy and told her so. She diagnosed my problem from Song of Solomon 2:5—"I am sick with love." I proposed marriage, and she accepted.

On New Year's Eve 1940, we made the announcement of our engagement in the Trotmans' newly acquired home in Hollywood. Mostly sailors were in attendance. We never did anything in those days without the support of Scripture, so I unromantically and insensitively quoted Job 3:25: "For the thing which I greatly feared is come upon me, and that which I was afraid of is come unto me."

Our engagement party was interrupted by the birth of the Trotmans' second daughter, Faith, that same evening.

We purchased a marriage license, expecting to be married when the ship returned to the mainland a few weeks later. But war clouds in the Pacific kept delaying the ship's return indefinitely. Morena's prolonged stay with the Trotmans finally ended when Dawson's money jar had accumulated $40 cash. In July 1941 he emptied the jar, which held all the money the household had. With it he bought Morena a ticket to Honolulu on the luxury liner *Matsonia*.

We arranged to be married at our favorite conference center at Kokokahi across the Pali on the north side of Oahu. The afternoon before the wedding, I picked up the marriage license at the bureau. The clerk asked where we were going to use it. When I told her Kokokahi, she said, "This license is not good there. It is only good in the judicial district of the city of Honolulu."

I panicked. There was a three-day waiting period before the license we needed was valid. The time for the wedding was only a few hours away. The clerk let me stew a few minutes and then said, "This happens often. You will have to have two weddings." She showed me a map. The closest geographical location to Kokokahi where we could use the license was the Pali, one of Hawaii's most famous tourist attractions. (The Pali is the mountain pass where the wind blows so strongly people have jumped over the cliff and landed safely below, being gently buoyed downward by the force of the wind.)

I phoned Morena, the preacher, and the best man, and we had the marriage ceremony standing beside the road with 45-mile-an-hour wind gusts. Later that evening, on July 11, 1941, we were married again by Navigator representative Harold DeGroff. The altar was covered with orchids for which we paid $10. The bill for the 55-guest banquet was $55.

Just 149 days later, our lives were interrupted by the Japanese attack on Pearl Harbor. I lost everything I owned except the clothes on my back. The only money we had was the change in Morena's purse. On Christmas day, Morena left Hawaii on a passenger liner turned military transport. We would not see each other face-to-face for the next 18 months.[1]

Our story is but one of the many brought about by Dawson and Lila's matchmaking. Many of us are still enjoying the results of their hard work.

---

[1] More details about my experience at Pearl Harbor are available online at www.usswestvirginia.com. Go to "Stories," and find "My Story by James Downing." See Chapters 5 and 6.

CHAPTER 8

A Yielded Life

AS WORLD WAR II DREW TO AN END, we decided to have a conference for the military men who had been involved in Navigator ministry. Plans were made for two such gatherings, one on each coast. Because I was stationed in Washington, D.C., I was responsible for the East Coast conference. The main speakers were Dawson Trotman and Jack Wyrtzen of Word of Life ministries.

Dawson arrived by train from California. Morena and I picked him up at Union Station and took him out to dinner. After a few minutes of visiting, I was amazed that Dawson was so different from the man we had known the past 13 years. His characteristic aggressiveness had been replaced by a deep mellowness. We noticed a new dimension of maturity, quietness, and depth of character.

Forgetting about the food, I said, "You are not the man we have known all these years. Something has happened to you. What is it?"

"You're right," he confirmed. "I am not the same man you have always known. Something has happened to me."

He proceeded to tell us about what may well have been the most important experiences of his Christian life.

He said he periodically had problems he couldn't solve with God alone. He had three trusted counselors—Dr. Charles Fuller of the *Old Fashioned Revival Hour* broadcast, Dr. Louis Talbot, president of the Bible Institute of Los Angeles, and "Daddy" Moon, a lay Bible teacher and scholar.

"But all of these men are 65 years of age or older," Dawson said. "I am 40 years old. Do I have to wait until I am 65 for God to use me in others' lives the way He uses these men in mine?"

He told the Lord, "I want to be that kind of man now."

He continued, "Outwardly I didn't place any restrictions on God. But deep in my heart I did. My secret prayer was, 'God, in accomplishing this, please don't touch my family or my good name.' "

I knew that Dawson was very proud of his family. In his eyes, they were the brightest and most beautiful on earth. (Groups of unmarried servicemen sometimes got a little weary of his boasting about his family, although none doubted the truthfulness of his assertions.)

In 1945, just months before our meeting in Washington, D.C., Dawson and Lila's fifth child was born. He was named Charles after Dawson's father. He was healthy, beautiful, and responsive for the first six weeks of his life. Then something happened. Dawson's theory was that while undergoing a six-week checkup, Chuckie might have been dropped and incurred brain damage.

From that day forward, his growth was stunted mentally and physically. Until Dawson's death, Chuckie wore diapers, ate baby food, and lived in a cradle at the foot of Dawson and Lila's bed. He never learned to talk or recognize anyone. He slept more in the daytime than at night and often wakened Dawson and Lila with his "gurgling" sounds. After Dawson's death, Chuckie was institutionalized and lived until the age of 16.

Dawson told us, "It is not easy to stand up on Sunday mornings and tell people how great God is and then go home to that child at the foot of our bed." He associated his boy's condition with his earlier prayer about his family. (The theology of this application may be questionable.)

Around this same time, one of the Navy men who had been a leader in the ministry began pointing out to Dawson some of the deficiencies he perceived in Dawson's life and character. Dawson graciously responded, confessed, and wrote letters of apology. But the accuser was not satisfied. He obtained a copy of the Navigator mailing list and sent a four-page letter to the entire Navigator constituency. It was signed by him and several other well-known Christians. In the letter, among other things, he accused Dawson of unrepentant pride and arrogance, dishonesty in handling finances, and indiscretions involving his wife.

Some thought this signaled the end of The Navigators. My counsel to him was not to take the matter so seriously. Hardly anyone impacted by Dawson Trotman was neutral about him. People either liked or disliked him with passion, and I had no doubt about the support of his loyal and grateful followers.

But Dawson took it hard. He said, "I never thought I would see the day I would have such a humiliating experience. As I walked to my office, BIOLA students crossed the street rather than walk on the same sidewalk with me."

Dawson's application was that the two areas of his life not totally yielded—his family and his good name—were now exposed. In the process of dealing with them, God extended his influence beyond a few thousand military men to make him a world influencer.

His three primary counselors and friends, Fuller, Talbot, and Moon, sent a follow-up letter to the Navigator constituency reassuring them that they had investigated the accusations and found them to be groundless.

Although these incidents were a mere ripple in Dawson's overall life, they had powerful effects on him. They also demonstrated the promise he often claimed from Isaiah 54:17, "No weapon that is formed against thee shall prosper; and every tongue that shall rise against thee in judgment thou shalt condemn."

Heavenbound at 50

DURING MIDWEEK OF THE THIRD WEEK of June 1956, Lila Trotman and three staff girls stopped for an evening visit at our home in Virginia Beach. They were en route to Schroon Lake, New York, where they would attend a weeklong conference. Dawson was the main speaker. Also attending would be Ruth Trotman, Waldron Scott, Joyce Turner, LeRoy Eims, and about a hundred other conferees. I was scheduled to arrive Tuesday morning with Ross Baldwin, director of the Servicemen's Center in Portsmouth, Virginia.

Dawson had been speaking at Park Street Church in Boston, and he and Lila were reunited at Schroon Lake. One of their main discussions there was to go over plans arising from the recent engagement of their older daughter, Ruth, to George Wortley.

Lila also brought Dawson up-to-date on her travels and visit with us in Virginia Beach. He asked about our 5-year-old twins, Donald and David, whom he had become especially fond of during his stay with us in Honolulu in 1953. After hearing about them from Lila, he put two one-dollar bills in an envelope and mailed them to us with a note to buy "junk," meaning candy, for the twins. Dawson's weekly pay at that time was $11 per week. The letter was delivered three days after he went home to be with the Lord.

During their time together Sunday afternoon, Lila brought up a serious conversation with Dawson. She told him she had a strong premonition that his life might end and that his death might be associated with water. She believed it was possible that the next time he took an overseas trip, the plane would go down and he would not survive. She wanted his input on many family and other matters while he was still available.

43

Dawson had no such premonition but entered into the spirit of the conversation. For four hours, Lila took shorthand notes of their conversation. Dawson not only answered her questions but also gave her messages for various friends and staff members. Lila never revealed the full scope of these messages, but she did reveal Dawson's message for Lorne Sanny. It was from Philippians 2:20—"For I have no man likeminded, who will naturally care for your state."

Ross and I drove all night and arrived at Schroon Lake at 6:30 Tuesday morning. A heavy pall silenced the camp. No one was stirring. I spotted a conferee having a quiet time. I interrupted him, saying, "Is this a Navigator conference? If it is, it is the deadest Navigator conference I have ever seen."

Soberly, he replied, "It may have something to do with the accident yesterday."

"What accident?"

"A man drowned."

"Who was it?"

"I don't know, but he seemed to be in charge around here."

"Was it Dawson Trotman?" I asked.

"Yes. That was his name. How did you know?"

I told my companion, Ross, "Excuse me. I have to walk this off." I had come to Schroon Lake to make final arrangements to leave the Navy and begin a new chapter of colaborship with Dawson, but that conversation would never happen.

Unfamiliar with the camp, my walk ended at the waterfront. About the time I got there, my deeply grieved friend Jack Wyrtzen arrived in his speedboat. He invited me to breakfast so he could tell me about the events of the previous day.

Jack Wyrtzen, whose Word of Life ministries owned the conference center at Schroon Lake, spent his summers on the property. During Monday afternoon's free time, he invited Dawson to take a ride with him in his five-passenger speedboat. When they got to the dock, several conferees were relaxing there. Generous Dawson, always wanting to serve, invited some of them along for the ride. Norman Larson got in the front seat with Jack. Three girls got in the rear seat. Dawson and the other two girls perched on the back of the rear seat with their feet behind the three seated girls.

Always cautious, Dawson inquired if there was anyone in the boat who couldn't swim. One of the girls was not a swimmer. Dawson locked arms with her on his left and the other girl on his right.

With eight people in the five-passenger boat, they sped out on the lake. A little more than a mile from land, Jack turned his head toward Dawson. Above the noise of the motor, he shouted, "Isn't this fun? Let's go get Lila." Dawson nodded. Jack applied full rudder to turn the boat around. The water was rough with some moderate waves. As the speeding boat began a sharp turn, it slapped into a wave with such force that from their high center of gravity, Dawson and the girl on his left, Allene Beck, were thrown overboard.

Dawson was a good swimmer. He knew Allene couldn't swim, so he began treading water while holding her to the surface. Jack threw some life jackets into the water and circled the boat back to Dawson and Allene. Those on board pulled Allene from his arms. The instant she was freed, Dawson's arms drifted apart, and he began to sink.

One of the girls in the boat was a skilled swimmer and experienced lifeguard. She dove overboard and got under Dawson to bring him to the surface. Then, for the first time in her life, she developed severe leg and stomach cramps. To save her own life, she had to let go of him. Jack then headed the boat to the dock to get help.

Lila had gone into the small town near the lake to purchase some groceries for her daughter Ruth, who was on a special diet. Driving back to camp, she developed such a heavy heart that she pulled over to the side of the road to pray about her premonition. Her main prayer was that when the time came, the Lord would give her the strength to be a good testimony.

Arriving back at the dock, Jack insisted that someone tell Lila. Dottie (McCutcheon) Anderson said she knew where Lila was staying and ran to tell her. She arrived at the cabin the same time Lila did. Dottie told Lila, "Dawson has fallen overboard, and they haven't found him yet." Amazingly, Lila replied, "I know."

45

Because Lila and I were old friends and the same age, I spent time with her daily. She remained at Schroon Lake for the entire week. Among other things, I learned the moment she pulled off the road to pray was the exact moment Dawson fell overboard.

The sheriff's office sent a search party to try to recover Dawson's body. They were unsuccessful after two days of searching. There was no sense of closure with the body missing, so much prayer was offered that the divers would be successful. A diver who had come to the area on another search read about Dawson's drowning and volunteered to help. He was taken to the approximate spot and located the body on his first dive. Some thought Dawson may have suffered a heart attack in the cold water, but the autopsy revealed that the cause of death was drowning.

The conference continued without Dawson. I was asked to take one of the sessions he had planned to lead. Lorne Sanny arrived Wednesday and took some of the other sessions.

Lila's prayer was granted. She was such a radiant testimony that a counselor sent out by the county to help her said, "She doesn't need what I have. I need what that lady has."

Although the conferee I saw early Tuesday morning had referred to the drowning as an "accident," I never heard that word again all week. The circumstances were so unusual that the events had to fall under the sovereignty of God.

The paradox of Dawson's death was lost on no one. The next issue of *TIME* magazine devoted its religious section to Dawson. The caption under his picture read, "Always holding someone up."

In his first communication after the death of Dawson Trotman, Lorne Sanny wrote in a Dear Gang letter:

"Monday afternoon I was in Tulsa, Oklahoma, for a rally with the Billy Graham team. Rod, Addie, and Millie phoned to tell me that the Lord had seen fit to take Dawson home. Of course, I was stunned. When I informed Billy a few minutes later, his first reaction was, "I can't believe it." Then as we talked further in his room, he said several times, "Oh God, I want to rededicate my life!"

Billy would later say that if we had sat down and planned the way God might take Dawson home, we certainly couldn't have conceived any more appropriate way than that he whose life was given to help others should be taken saving another. Billy also told Lorne, "You just count me as a member of your staff. I will go anywhere or do anything you ask."

For the only time in his crusade history, Billy turned over the preaching to an associate and left the crusade in Oklahoma to conduct Dawson's memorial service in Colorado.

Some people thought of Dawson Trotman's homegoing at age 50 as a tragedy. This conclusion is debatable.

During his Honolulu visit with us in 1953, 47-year-old Dawson and I talked about his future and the future of The Navigators. He said that with the Billy Graham team, he had been wined and dined around the world. He'd been in governors' mansions and had tea with the Queen, and he had no further desire to travel or take on new projects. He just wanted to spend the rest of his life keeping in touch with the 60 or so men—of which I was one, he said—in whose lives he had invested. He wanted to be sure they were still carrying out the things he had taught them.

About The Navigators, he said he had made his contribution. Trained men were in place, ready to take over just as soon as he got out of the way. He acknowledged he was a "bottleneck" to growth and expansion.

I didn't take the conversation seriously at the time. But after his unexpected promotion to heaven in 1956, I reflected back on his comments.

Billy Graham said at his memorial service that Dawson had lived more in 50 years than many people live in a lifetime. Like John the Baptist, he was not a shining light but a *burning* light. During the last year of his life, Dawson's physical, emotional, and mental energy had peaked and was on the decline. (Of course, spiritual adrenaline helped him with the tasks at hand.) During his last months at Glen Eyrie, his executive assistant Dorothy Anderson noticed that he could only muster the strength to spend an hour or so a day taking care of urgent and routine matters at his office. On one of his last trips,

Dawson followed one of his established customs of dictating and sending tapes to his office to be transcribed. Even though Dorothy was very familiar with his voice and thought processes, his weak voice and somewhat incoherent thoughts in those final tapes could not be transcribed. Like David, he had served God's purpose for his generation and was ready to enter his eternal reward.

There seems to be a common profile among entrepreneurial types like Dawson Trotman. They are visionary, are unrealistic about finances, and find it difficult to delegate.

As Betty Skinner pointed out in *DAWS,* Dawson was threatened by strong men close to him and held them at arm's length.

Perhaps God was so determined that the Navigator ministry increase and multiply that He did not intervene in the natural events on Schroon Lake that day in 1956. He changed leadership according to His schedule. Soon The Navigators would learn the meaning of "team leadership" as discovered and implemented by Lorne Sanny. Lorne knew how to exploit the strengths of strong men who were driven by the Navigator vision. Under his leadership, The Navigators would grow tenfold and then a hundredfold.

PART II

Lorne Sanny

INTRODUCTION

FOR TWO YEARS PRIOR TO LORNE'S promotion to heaven, I had been working on this manuscript with the working title of *Thirty Years at the Right Hand of Two Great Men.* I showed Lorne all of the chapters about Dawson and several about him. I asked for his comments as to what I should add, correct, or delete. His reply: "Don't change a thing except the title." He was not comfortable being called a great man, although to me, he was just that.

In one of our last in-depth conversations, I asked Lorne what he thought he would be most remembered for. He thought it would probably be as a leader. He was quick to follow up, "But I am not a leader or even a pioneer. My role has been that of a sheepdog nipping here and there to keep some strong men moving together in the right direction."

There may be more truth than jest in one of his favorite stories: When Mahatma Ghandi was India's leader, he and a guest were taking a late-evening walk. As is so prevalent in that part of the world, multitudes of other people were also walking. Ghandi's guest said to him, "Where are all these people going?" He responded, "I don't know, but I guess I should find out because I am their leader."

This helps explain Lorne's objectives in visiting field ministries. He would say, "I try to observe what God is blessing in an area and then pass it along to others."

A Nav rep once asked a visiting Lorne, "What are your objectives for this area?" Lorne proceeded to set him straight. "What I want to know," he replied, "is what are *your* objectives for this area?"

Lorne believed that a leader needed to be a pioneer. Because he was not an innovator in ministry skills and techniques, he felt he was not really a leader. But with his skill at "exploiting the strengths of strong men," he was successful at accomplishing the mission of The Navigators. In this way, he was not unlike Napoléon, who has been called the greatest military and political leader of all time. Retired British Lieutenant General D.E. Hoste said that Napoléon surrounded himself with a council of men characterized by strengths in areas in which he knew he was weak. Lorne's ability to do this made him a successful leader.

Meeting Lorne Sanny

IN 1940, THE PACIFIC FLEET, of which my ship, the USS *West Virginia,* was a part, changed its home port from Long Beach, California, to Pearl Harbor, Hawaii. Our contact with Dawson Trotman and the home office was by mail. In 1941, the name of Lorne Sanny began to appear frequently in newsletters. It was evident this young man was filling a strategic role at the headquarters and in local ministry.

On December 25, 1941, following the attack on Pearl Harbor, my wife, Morena, and other dependents of military personnel were sent back to the mainland. Back in the States, Morena headed for Little Rock, Arkansas, to be with her family. Along the way, she stopped at the Trotman home for a visit. Someone took a picture of all the guests there that evening. Included in this picture was a boyish-looking 21-year-old young man, Lorne Sanny. After seeing the picture, I was able to attach a face to a familiar name.

Our first face-to-face meeting wouldn't come until several years later, in the spring of 1956. Dawson and Lila were participating in a Billy Graham crusade in Richmond, Virginia. I was stationed on a ship at Norfolk, about a hundred miles from Richmond, so Dawson invited Morena and me, along with Lester and Martha Spencer, to join them at their hotel for a two-day visit. During this stay, I was introduced to various people on the Graham team, including a very busy young man, Lorne Sanny, who had led the counselor training and was now leading the follow-up team.

Another important event in my life occurred during that visit. Dawson engaged me in an extremely serious conversation. He was confident it was time for me to leave the Navy and join his team full-time. I reminded him that about 18 years earlier we'd had a similar conversation. After much prayer and deliberation, we felt at that time I could best serve the ministry of The Navigators by being a career man inside the Navy. I reminded him that day at the hotel that I was having a fruitful ministry, was at the height of my career, and was about to receive a promotion in rank that included command of a larger ship. Morena and the family loved our spacious country home near Virginia Beach with its large trees, big front yard, garden, and pony stable.

As always, Dawson was quick on the mental and spiritual trigger, quoting John 15:2, "Every branch in Me that beareth not fruit he taketh away: and every branch that beareth fruit, he purgeth it, that it may bring forth more fruit."

After the evening crusade meeting, Dawson had the staff arrange a special dinner with Lorne and the team to introduce Morena and me. He publicly announced that it was imperative we join the staff full-time and that if it were a matter of finances, he would consider going to work to contribute to our support. I don't think anyone took him seriously, but he had made his point very persuasively.

My next meeting with Lorne was a few weeks later, June 20, 1956, under humanly tragic circumstances.

After the Richmond meeting, Morena and I had continued to pray and concluded it was time to retire from my 24-year Navy career and join The Navigators full-time. I arranged to meet Dawson at a conference in upper New York to tell him the news and work out the timing and details of this new arrangement. Of course, that conversation never happened.

After hearing of Dawson's death, Lorne turned over his responsibilities at a Billy Graham crusade in Oklahoma to join us at Schroon Lake. At the end of the week, Lorne left the conference to meet Dan Piatt, the Navigator European director who was arriving in New York City by ship. Lorne suggested I make the six-hour trip with him.

During the drive, he shared with me that he knew he would one day inherit the job of leading The Navigators. Suddenly, that day had arrived for 35-year-old Lorne. He had already decided that instead of it being a one-man operation, it would be a team operation. He told me that the Lord had given him the names of the men to be on the team, and I was one of them. He was aware of the persuasive pressure Dawson had put on me to come on board full-time, and he repeated the invitation with renewed urgency.

Dawson had written me a four-page letter detailing what he had in mind for me as a full-time staff, but I wasn't sure what Lorne might be thinking. I asked him what he expected me to do. It wasn't clear to him, he said, but he believed the Lord was prompting him to have me on the team in some capacity. During the six-hour conversation, one thing on his mind came through crystal clear. It was Glen Eyrie. To Dawson it was more than a headquarters, conference center, and training facility. It was sort of a Christian theme park. He loved to travel through the grounds in his convertible and communicate by shortwave radio as his active imagination thought of new ways to beautify, improve, and utilize this God-given facility.

To Lorne, at that point in time, Glen Eyrie was one giant "white elephant"—a valuable possession whose upkeep exceeded its usefulness. (In his later years, Lorne's views radically changed, and he gave considerable time and effort to perpetuate the Glen's ministry.) My first job would be to take the responsibility for Glen Eyrie off his hands.

Toward the conclusion of our talk and after discussing many possibilities, Lorne used an illustration from baseball. He said coaches and managers have what they call "utility outfielders." They are capable of playing several positions and fill in whenever and wherever there is a need. Lorne asked me to join his team as a utility player to help him wherever he saw the greatest need.

This was the beginning of a day-to-day relationship with the greatest man I have ever known. Lorne Sanny was mature, wise, intelligent, and transparent. His pursuit of holiness was a model for all of us to follow. He was disciplined, shrewd, teachable, fair, compassionate, and a master in human relations. I would spend the next 22 years seeing firsthand what made this remarkable man tick.

Joining Lorne's Team

I NEXT SAW LORNE AT DAWSON'S memorial service at Glen Eyrie. Morena and I took turns driving straight through from Norfolk to Colorado Springs. This was our first visit to Glen Eyrie; we were able to find it from pictures in the brochure we had seen.

There was little time for visiting. On June 27, 1956, we participated in a service at the Pink House in which Billy Graham led the leaders of some 30 Christian organizations in laying hands on Lorne and dedicating him for his new task as president of The Navigators.

After returning home and reflecting on my time with Lorne, I wrote him a letter in early September, outlining what I felt were the immediate priorities for The Navigators. These were in the areas of financial stability, a clear statement of mission and objectives, and a strategy for accomplishing our purposes. He agreed in principle and again urged me to hasten my transition.

The Navy released me at midnight on Sunday, October 31, 1956. On Monday morning, we loaded our two cars with suitcases and six children and headed for Colorado Springs. I left the family with my parents in Missouri, and on Thursday, I entered Glen Eyrie for the second time. Within a few days, I had purchased a three-bedroom house in Colorado Springs for $18,000. The mortgage interest rate was 3½ percent, and the monthly payments were $123. I returned to Missouri to pick up the family and then checked in for duty at the headquarters office.

The first observation I made was that Lorne seemed to be as emotionally and psychologically attached to the Billy Graham team as to The Navigators. Being in charge of their counselor training and follow-up program fit well with his gifts of communication, teaching, organizing, innovating, and public relations. He was clearly his own man after years of being an insider on the Graham team. Those were days of great personal fulfillment; I believe he considered them the most rewarding of his life. It would be three years before he would sever his ties with the Graham team.

I next discovered that Dawson had felt the need to recruit to the staff older men who had not grown up in the Navigator family. I was given a desk and chair in the loft of the headquarters building— later known as the International Office—which already housed three such men. Besides Dick Hightower, a long-time Navigator, there were Jack Mayhall, recruited from his role as youth pastor of Portland Bible Church; George Sanchez, recruited from radio station HCJB; and medical doctor Lewis Bock, who left his practice to join The Navigators. Because we were all older—I was 43 at the time—I dubbed the loft the "den of antiquity."

None of us had a job description. As far as I could determine, we also had no vital function or regular contact with Lorne, who was preoccupied with many details when he was not on the road with the Graham team. I feared the worst. In spite of our conversations and correspondence, there seemed to be no real job.

After a few days of idleness, I decided to take initiative in two areas. Lorne had previously asked me to take Glen Eyrie off his hands, so I decided to start there. The door to the main entrance of the office had a thin veneer strip covering it. Years of weather and moisture had caused it to fade and wrinkle. It gave a terrible first impression to those entering the office. I asked Dick Snell, who had the title "Glen Eyrie foreman," if he could find enough money to purchase a new door.

"I bought a new door eight months ago," he said. "It's stored in the shop."

"Why hasn't it been installed?" I asked.

"I'm waiting for Lorne to pick out the kind of hinges and doorknob he wants," Dick answered.

I asked the obvious question. "Does Lorne want to select the hardware for the door?"

"Dawson would have, so I assume Lorne does."

I then said, "Dick, you impress me as having pretty good taste. Why don't you pick out the hardware and install the door. If Lorne asks you why you didn't check with him, tell him I told you to do it."

As the new kid on the block, I thought I may have overstepped my bounds. The next time I saw Lorne, I told him what I had done. That conversation helped me know Lorne better. Someone had told him, "If you take care of the details, the big things will take care of themselves." He took that advice seriously.

After a brief mental struggle about the front-door hardware, he said, "It's OK. Let Dick go ahead."

After that incident, Dick Snell accepted me as Lorne's representative for Glen Eyrie, and we got along fine.

I had no regular contact with Lorne, and I was somewhat frustrated about other things urgently needing attention. I had read in *TIME* magazine about how General Gruenther, General Eisenhower's chief of staff at NATO headquarters, communicated with him. He sent him short memos called "Gruenther grams." (General Eisenhower would never read a memo more than a half-page long. He felt any communications longer than a half-page had not been thought through and a conclusion and recommendation reached.) So I wrote a memo to Lorne telling him I was going to originate a series of "Jimgrams" on matters I felt strongly about.

As he received these memos, he would call me in for further discussion. More often than not, my solution was accepted or modified, and I inherited the responsibility for implementing it. One of the biggest needs I saw for improvement was in our financial management. He responded by making me financial vice president, which was the first administrative title I held.

Although I had Lorne's total backing, gaining acceptance into a decision-making role was not easy. Part of it was philosophical. To me, The Navigators was a group of men and women on the front-lines, waging spiritual warfare, releasing captives out of darkness, and equipping them and enlisting them in spiritual battle. I did not easily comprehend how a headquarters operation fit into the battle. Lorne was focused on mass evangelism with the Graham team, and the office staff and Glen Eyrie crews were still bathing in the euphoria of having secured Glen Eyrie years earlier. They had attained their Navigator Nirvana and were basking in its sunlight.

I was an outsider who had to be careful not to disobey my wife's version of the eleventh commandment: "Thou shalt not rock the boat."

Gradually, and with Lorne's complete support, I became recognized as his representative to the headquarters staff. My routine soon became meeting one by one with the seven lead men and women for a half-hour every day. These were the people responsible for the office and Glen Eyrie staff.

Securing Glen Eyrie with the miraculous provision of money at the eleventh hour had been a glorious event. But there is another side of the story. To set up Glen Eyrie as a fully functioning headquarters, conference center, and training facility required more than the purchase price of $340,000. The amount owed to local suppliers and tradesmen at the time of Dawson's death was $36,865.69. (At Dawson's public memorial service, held at the First Methodist Church, Bob Pierce, president and founder of World Vision, took the initiative to raise about $25,000 to cover some of that debt. In the following days, Billy Graham was extremely helpful in using his name to raise additional money to apply toward the debt.)

The Navigators' credit rating in the community was zero. If a vendor delivered food, gasoline, or other material, he would stop by the Bookkeeping Department and pick up a check before unloading. Bookkeeping maintained a list of our creditors and the amount we owed them. It was four pages long, single-spaced. Each month in which we generated even a small surplus, it was used to pay off one or more of the creditors.

Dawson's perfectionism had not carried over into his administrative leadership. One of the lead men I met with daily was Harvey Oslund. Dawson had recruited this young businessman, a Navy veteran, to come to Glen Eyrie and set up a print shop. Harv did a good job, but I was somewhat irritated by his constant bugging of people in the other six departments. One day I asked Harv why he was always telling other department heads how to do their jobs.

He answered, "Because I am supposed to."

I asked him to explain what he meant.

He described the following environment: All of the office crew had meals together at the Castle. Dawson was generally with them for lunch. If a person happened to step out of the office at the same time Dawson did and walked to the Castle with him, it made their day.

One day Harv had the good fortune to harmonize his departure with Dawson's. When they arrived at the Castle, Dawson said to him, "Harv, between the office and the Castle, we passed six things that were wrong and need correcting. What I want to know is, what were the six, and what are you going to do about them?"

When Dawson took one of his frequent trips, he never specifically left anyone in charge. When he returned and saw something wrong, he was apt to have an instruction session with the first person he saw. Hence, everyone felt responsible for trying to correct any situation that might create Dawson's displeasure. And his tastes were not always predictable. One of the memos I saw from Dawson to the gang asked them not to take shortcuts between buildings when there was snow on the ground. He asked that they stick to the road lest their footprints mar the beauty of the snow-covered landscape.

(Lorne used to talk about the time he and Dawson visited someone's home. After they had departed and were well on their way, Dawson asked Lorne to describe the landscaping, including the type and color of flowers in the yard. I have to believe this idiosyncrasy was really an effort to get people to be fully observant.)

Dawson's standards lingered on after his death, as I found out when I violated one. Four parking spaces were reserved in the office parking lot for some of us who had offices there. They were much more spacious than ordinary parking spaces with plenty of room on either side. I had a habit, particularly when in a hurry, of not parking exactly parallel to the lines. Looking back, I can see how it made the parking lot look sloppy. One day, Lorne asked me to preserve the symmetry and park my car like the others. His lack of enthusiasm in exhorting me led me to believe he was honoring a complaint of others in the office. Months after Dawson's death, they still felt his piercing eyes and scowling brow looking down from heaven for allowing such an unsightly practice.

Exploiting the Strengths of Others

As Lorne grew in his role as president, he began maximizing his skill of harnessing and utilizing the strengths of the people around him. He and the other men who had worked under Dawson had grown up in the "everyone-responsible-for-everything" environment, and Lorne allowed that to continue for a while. But eventually, instead of holding them at a distance, Lorne began exploiting the strengths of those on his team. Dawson had most of the Nav reps report directly to him, but Lorne began to put out the word that staff would report to the one in charge of their ministry or department. He once said, "I leave a man in his job long enough to live with his mistakes."

Lorne first empowered the new vice president, Bob Foster, who was asked to move from California to Colorado Springs, where he led the Navigator ministry thrust for the next year and a half. Gradually, Lorne began empowering others, including Rod Sargent, Doug Sparks, Waldron Scott, and Jim Petersen.

Rod's skills were in the area of public relations and fund-raising. At age 62, his body ravaged with cancer, he still worked long hours. Many of the projects he worked so passionately for still stand as monuments of his hard work.

Doug Sparks was a Navy veteran rich with overseas experience. Except for Latin America, the overseas ministry of today is an extension of Doug's work. He single-handedly established the European and Middle East and African ministries and added his stamp of authenticity to the Asia Navigator ministry.

Lorne appreciated colaboring with Waldron "Scotty" Scott, who added an important dimension to the team. He was a master of contrary opinion who saw to it that every side of the issue at hand was thoroughly considered. His vast knowledge of missions history and his own successful pioneering ministry overseas made him a valuable member of Lorne's team.

After Scotty left the team, Jim Petersen took his place as the one who advocated alternate views. After visiting Jim in Brazil, Lorne wrote, "Jim is a real leader, a man of imagination, a thinker, and a man with a lot of drive."

In addition to these gifted men, Lorne also had the partnership of Jack Mayhall, LeRoy Eims, and Skip Gray, who were architects of the U.S. collegiate ministry, and George Sanchez, who served skillfully as overseas director. These are just some of the individuals who worked with Lorne on a day-to-day, face-to-face basis.

Trials of a New President

IN THE EARLY DAYS OF HIS PRESIDENCY, Lorne publicly referred to himself as the "reluctant leader." Sometimes after a challenging staff meeting, Lorne would say, "I don't want to be the president. I just want to be one of the guys." Sometimes Lorne would ask me to chair staff meetings so he could participate in the discussion of issues. One time when he thought the discussion was ready for conclusion and decision, he interjected, "I vote this way." I later pointed out, "Lorne, you realize your vote was a very big vote."

But this "reluctant leader" never doubted that the Lord had given him that responsibility. That assurance was not universal.

One staff member—a peer of Lorne's—had become a Christian while in the Navy and was a favorite of Dawson's. He was handsome, charismatic, articulate, a great communicator, and an influencer of others. He had been given major responsibilities, including teaching Navigator basics at Northwestern Bible College when Billy Graham was president there. Along with Lorne, he was active in Billy Graham campaigns. Some of the staff felt he was a natural to succeed Dawson.

Another prime candidate was Doug Sparks. His drive, powerful communication skills, ministry-mindedness, and claiming of promises echoed Dawson Trotman. He had the spirit and creativity of a pioneer but was also an accomplished leader and administrator. But Doug was so involved in The Navigators' worldwide work that it seemed best for him to remain where he was.

Even Lila had the vote of at least one person, a rich widow, world-class businesswoman, and generous supporter of The Navigators. She was a close friend of the Trotmans and a chief source of support for Lila after Dawson's death. There was little doubt in her mind that Lila was to be Dawson's successor. She immediately gave Lila the title of cofounder of The Navigators and became a public advocate in her favor.

This wonderful lady also gave low-profile Lorne the impression that he had no right to be president. My most fervent prayer sessions with Lorne were as he tried to cope with this stressful situation.

There was also the opinion of ex-military men who came out of the "decade of disciplemaking." Many of them were in positions of leadership in the missionary and Christian world. At a reunion at Glen Eyrie, a group of them met with Lorne and in no uncertain terms let him know that although he held the office of president, they considered Jim Downing to be Dawson's successor.

Whenever I heard people discussing the wisdom of the board of director's decision to make Lorne president, my reply was—and still is—"The board of directors did not select Lorne; the Lord did." I never doubted this during the years I partnered and fellowshipped with him.

As part of Dawson's team, Lorne had held the title of vice president and occupied the office closest to Dawson's. The headquarters staff had such respect for Lorne they accepted him unconditionally, even though his work with the Billy Graham team kept him less involved in Navigator ministry than they were.

Carrying Out Another Man's Vision

Lorne once asked Dawson, "How do you maintain a vision for working with men?" He was asking about the individual effort and intensity required to raise up reproducing men and women to help fulfill the Great Commission.

Dawson replied, "Sometimes I wonder if you really have it."

But Lorne did have it, as those of us who worked with him know well.

A few weeks after I came to Glen Eyrie, I asked Lorne what would happen if The Navigators shifted to a more conventional ministry and slacked away from Dawson's vision of raising up reproducing laborers. Lorne's reply was crystal clear: "The Navigators would cease to exist."

Lorne's talent, brilliance, determination, gifts, communication skills, and character ensured his success in any endeavor he might have pursued. Multitudes are grateful and blessed that he chose to surrender his own ambition in order to perpetuate another man's vision to new generations.

Despite his patience and graciousness, there was one phrase Lorne grew weary of. It was, "If Dawson were here, this is what he would do." With righteous indignation, Lorne would reply, "Listen, I worked alongside Dawson Trotman for 15 years, and I never could predict what he was going to do in the next five minutes. Don't tell me that you know what he would do now."

The Glen Eyrie Community

ONE OF THE MOST POSITIVE THINGS Lorne inherited was the Glen Eyrie community. Such close fellowship was a delight few people have the privilege of enjoying this side of heaven.

All of the single men and women, along with the married couples without children, lived on the property. They ate three meals a day together in the Castle dining room. Married couples who lived off-site were encouraged to bring their children to Glen Eyrie for Sunday dinner. These children grew up thinking of Glen Eyrie as their second home. Many of this second generation would later attend Eagle Lake Camp.

Of course, the staff had some challenges. Only a few—those who had an outside source of income—owned cars. The salary for those living on the Glen was $7.50 per week. Married couples not living on the Glen were paid $11 per family member per week. Morena and I had six children, so our pay was $88 weekly—an annual salary of $4,576. The Sannys also had six children, making us the highest-paid families in The Navigators. (The last paycheck Dawson Trotman drew was for $22.)

A critical decision had to be made every Friday: Who would be paid? The answer depended on how much money was in the bank. Families always received their pay, but sometimes the single men and women went without any cash for several weeks. On two different occasions, discharged servicemen who worked in Bookkeeping were so touched by the financial needs they gave all their savings to help the general fund.

The Navigators didn't offer a medical plan, retirement, Social Security, or other benefits. One month's pay was not enough for a doctor's visit, so we prayed for good health. Several Christian doctors in town lowered their fees or waved them altogether as their contribution to The Navigators.

In 1957, Lorne was heavily involved with a Billy Graham crusade in New York City. Roger Hull, chairman of the crusade, was president of Mutual of New York, a large insurance company. Because Lorne knew him personally, Mr. Hull's company was able to underwrite The Navigators' first corporate health-insurance policy in 1957. The Navigators paid the premiums, and this became the first staff benefit.

One of the first major decisions I recall Lorne making was to make funds for payroll a priority. He believed "the worker deserves his wages" (Luke 10:7, NIV). It proved to be a decision God honored; there was always enough money to make the payroll after that.

In the Carriage House basement was a missionary barrel. Local churches and compassionate individuals kept it stocked to clothe the Glen Eyrie family. Betty Skinner's mother, Miss Bess, kept a sewing bag near the missionary barrel so the men could extend the life of their garments. She also collected and ironed the men's shirts.

All the work on the property was done by the various crews. The only utility vehicle was an old pickup truck known as the Red Flash that came with the property. The 11 acres of lawn were mowed by hand-operated mowers. One day as I was visiting with one of the perspiring men mowing the grass, a military jet flew overhead. He looked up at it and said, "Sometimes I wonder why I left the program where I was flying jets to come to Glen Eyrie and run a lawnmower."

With so much old and broken-down equipment, the repair crews were kept busy. Of the several washing machines in the housing units, there wasn't even one that was reliable. I am sure the repairman spent much of his time praying for finances to buy new machines.

The Castle was not the majestic palace it is today. The floor was bare. There were practically no drapes on the windows. Many of the hand-painted tiles from the fireplaces were missing—chipped off as souvenirs by vandals who had broken into the Castle looking for adventure. Many of the Great Hall's oak panels were stained and warped from water leaks during the 27-year period the Castle went unused. Although equipped with beds, many of the rooms were more like a run-down barracks than premium accommodations.

The old laundry building, adjacent to the former International Office, was used for housing. One summer it was called the "couples apartments" when four couples were housed there. The wives slept upstairs and the husbands downstairs.

The roads and most of the parking lots were unpaved. The dust from the roads made housekeeping in all of the buildings a special chore.

Despite the conditions—and the rare instances of fornication or a "peeping tom"—the community was so hilariously happy that those who were part of it felt they were cheating on heaven.

The high point of the week was Glen Eyrie night. Every Thursday night, staff living both on and off the property gathered for two hours in the Pink House living room. Most sat on the floor. There were singing, testimonies, and refreshments, but most treasured were the announcements. Breaking news from the small Navigator world was shared, including any new assignments and news of staff engagements. Young couples only became engaged with the approval of the senior staff, who served as go-betweens, and there was great secrecy and many surprises. After the announcement by a senior staff, the couple told how the Lord had led in their developing relationship. When some of these announcements were made, other men and women sat in pained disbelief. They were sure the Lord had promised them one of the newly engaged.

It has been said that 50 to 60 percent of our energy is emotional energy, available only when we are excited about what we are doing and enjoying great pleasure from it. The adrenaline from a Glen Eyrie night lasted for the next three days. The anticipation of another one three days later was no doubt a factor in the almost superhuman weekly accomplishments pulled off by the Glen Eyrie and office crews.

In addition to their jobs, the staff attended training classes every week. Lorne approved the several courses taught in the training program. One leader proposed a course in Bible doctrine. Lorne disapproved, maintaining there is no such thing as isolating a few truths and categorizing them as Bible doctrine. He believed that we should study the whole Bible.

Another of Lorne's strong opinions was related to a five-day workweek. He insisted that the Bible said we were to work six days, not five. We compromised and gave our crews Wednesday afternoons off but worked a half-day on Saturdays.

Despite the staff's hard work, much creativity was exhibited by pranksters trying to outdo each other. One of the girls came from a wealthy background. Her father decorated the third-floor apartment in the Castle for her, complete with a television set. One day, some of the fellows got into her apartment and took off the back of the TV and put an alarm clock inside. It went off at four o'clock in the morning. She couldn't locate it to turn it off until she got help from a technician.

One Halloween, the cook saturated all the food with a yellow-green food coloring. It didn't affect the taste but had a psychological effect. Most of the food prepared for that night's dinner was fed to the pig we kept to eat the garbage. (The job assigned to the newest trainee was to feed the kitchen leftovers to the pig three times a day. When the pig was ready for market, it was sold and the proceeds financed a party.)

One of the Glen's best-kept secrets is that it is home to many rattlesnakes. In fact, the ridge to the south of the entrance is unofficially called Rattlesnake Ridge. One day, one of the trainees caught a small rattlesnake and felt compelled to educate some of the girls on how to recognize and deal with them. With the girls in a circle around him, he let the snake coil around his left arm. Holding its head in his left hand, he pointed out the fangs with his right index finger. The rattler lunged and clamped down on his finger. We rushed him to the hospital. The nurse phoned ahead to the hospital so they were prepared to properly treat him. He lost the end of his finger as an eternal reminder of his experience.

We prayed fervently that the press would not find out about the incident. Some of the local community wondered what kind of cult we were. Being branded as "snake handlers" would not have been helpful. Years earlier, Dawson and Lila had been given a promise from Isaiah 54:17: "No weapon that is formed against thee shall prosper; and every tongue that shall rise against thee in judgment thou shalt condemn. This is the heritage of the servants of the LORD, and their righteousness is of me, saith the LORD." One of the many miracles we have experienced is the way in which the Lord has protected the public image of The Navigators.

One morning each week, we all came to the Castle for a prayer meeting from 6:30 to 7:30. We met in small groups and then had breakfast together. I was in the same group as Bill Michael, our cook. I expected that Bill would leave the group at about 7:00 to get breakfast ready for us. When he was still praying at 7:25, I began preparing for a morning fast. About three minutes before 7:30, Bill went to the kitchen, plugged in the 12-slice toaster, and set out a few loaves of bread and some jam and jelly along with gallon containers of milk and juice. He then put a case of boxed cereal—he called them "munchy crunchies"—on the counter, and breakfast for 50 was served.

At some point, the staff became convinced that they could not have a quiet time without a desk and chair or a shelf to spread out their Bible and notebook. With the zeal of the "sooners" who homesteaded Oklahoma, they staked out every windowsill, stairwell, corner, cranny, and closet as a personal quiet-time altar. There was an unwritten understanding that no one trespass into another person's quiet-time location. When someone left the Glen and vacated their quiet-time nook, there was a mad rush to stake claim on it.

The universal excuse for not having a quiet time, both inside and outside The Navigators, seemed to be, "I don't have a place where I can go." Lorne mentioned to me one day that perhaps The Navigators should abandon all we were doing and go into the business of manufacturing and marketing "quiet-time booths."

Not all who came to Glen Eyrie had a complete orientation. After being at the Glen for two or three weeks, one of the girls was asked what she did in her morning quiet time. She answered honestly, "I wrote a letter and took a nap."

In the 1960s, a new innovation came into existence that rivaled Glen Eyrie night for hilarity and edification. It was the "hayloft opera." The present Timothy House was then a working horse barn, complete with all the smells. The hayloft became a small auditorium featuring music and skits. With Bob Vidano as emcee and LeRoy Eims as the star actor, the community enjoyed many hours of great music and homespun humor. Friends could come by invitation only, and it was a special feather in the cap to be included. Those who attended will never forget LeRoy's Mad Doctor and Old Maid skits, Selva Roark's horseback riding, Sam Clark's Marine general presentations, or Rod Sargent's humorous bridegroom drama.

To promote Glen Eyrie, we once decided we should make a film. We arranged for a professional scriptwriter to spend a week at the Glen to prepare him for the task. We never followed through on making the film. Perhaps we doubted the ability of the writer to portray what we had in mind. At the end of the week, he said, "Glen Eyrie is not a place; it is an emotion."

Hundreds—if not thousands—have developed a love affair with Glen Eyrie and expect it to be treated and cherished as well as any soul mate. This is especially true of its earliest Navigator residents.

Up to his last day, Lorne wanted to see Glen Eyrie fully endowed. He gave his name and final energy to raising funds so that Glen Eyrie could fulfill its purpose as a ministry center to the public and other Christian organizations, as well as a spiritual home and rallying place for Navigators and their friends.

Lorne's Headquarters Support

ALTHOUGH HE INHERITED PRIMITIVE equipment at the Glen, Lorne had a well-oiled and functioning administration there. Since his early years with The Navigators, Lorne's secretary was Millie Hopkins. She was so capable and had such an amenable personality and such capacity, she easily slipped into the role of president's executive assistant when Lorne took on his new role. She served with him until his retirement in 1986.

She always knew where to find the information Lorne needed. She understood Lorne so well that he could give her a few thoughts for a letter, and she could put it in his own words. This saved him a lot of time. She also knew how to guard confidences and protect his time. She was skilled in dealing with the public. She worked to improve her professional skills and set the standard for and trained other secretaries. She wielded the power inherent in her job with a low profile. Everyone loved and respected Millie.

Financial transactions, except for receipting, were all handled by the Bookkeeping Department. The only mechanical aids they used were typewriters and adding machines. All bookkeeping entries were made manually. The Receipting Department typed a receipt with carbon copies on a manual typewriter for each gift given. Donor records and entries were entered by hand on cards. The majority of income was used for headquarters needs. We did have a missionary fund, but for the most part, it was undesignated and was distributed according to the perceived need of our missionaries.

U.S. field representatives raised their own support and receipted their own donors. Our chief accountant instructed the staff: "You should not include in your income tax return any personally designated gift for which you gave a Navigator receipt so long as the money was not for services rendered." In the family-like atmosphere, Nav reps generously shared their income with other staff in need and friends of other organizations. This prompted a further warning about treating gifts from gift income as deductions: "A problem may arise from showing an income of, say $672, and claiming, say $600 in gifts to other individuals."

Some of my time was spent going to IRS offices with reps who had been called in to explain their somewhat mysterious tax returns. One examiner asked how he could get someone to give him tax-free income. (I did not extend to him an invitation to join our staff.) We were operating within existing law, so we were never overruled.

When I came to Glen Eyrie, Jerry Bridges was the very capable supervisor of the large Correspondence Department. It consisted of 18 to 20 workers and had two main functions. The largest operation was handling orders for Navigator materials, mainly the *Topical Memory System*. At that time, the TMS was a correspondence course. People were only given one-third of the verses at a time. After proving they had recited the verses without prompting—and giving the correct reference "fore and aft"—they were sent another section. The proof was a signed statement by the person who had listened to the recitation, often a pastor. This meant keeping an individual record card on each enrollee. Entries were made by hand. If a person did not respond in a reasonable period of time, they were sent a letter checking up on them.

(As a matter of interest, the highest completion was a group of inmates at the Idaho State Penitentiary. They were kept in their cells from 3:30 P.M. to 8:30 A.M., which facilitated a completion record of 94 percent. The chaplain of the prison had a Navigator background and encouraged participation. LeRoy Eims and I once spent a day with the Christian inmates there.)

The TMS was printed in Harvey Oslund's coal-bin print shop. The individual cards were printed in sheets and then cut into stacks of individual cards. The packets to hold the cards were also printed there and scored in sheets. Putting a memory pack together required handling every one of the cards and folding every pack-holder individually.

Collating and folding these cards by hand was a tedious, never-ending job. No one crew was assigned this task; rather, it was usually assigned to new trainees and called the "attitude tester." Their survival and attitudes sometimes determined their future with The Navigators.

When we got behind, whole crews were called in after hours to help catch up. Often guests spent their daytime hours as "volunteer" collators. Any family member was subject to the collating "draft," and any visiting friend who hinted they might want to help was pressed into TMS service.

The girls in the Correspondence Department who received these orders would type the customer's address on a shipping label. On the front of the label, they would type a code for the Shipping Department to decipher and ship the order. Thus, the *Topical Memory System* became the TMS, *Beginning with Christ*, BWC, *Going On with Christ,* GOWC. These code names were understood in house, but outsiders wondered what unknown tongue Navigators were speaking in.

It seemed impossible to keep up with the workload, and we often fell embarrassingly behind. One time, when Receipting was three weeks behind, I told the supervisor we couldn't continue to have all our donors unhappy because of late receipts. I told him to make at least a few happy by receipting for today's gifts first, then yesterday's, and so forth. Somehow, this sparked a new burst of energy, and in a few weeks, the backlog was cleared up. The goal of receipting gifts the same day was achieved and maintained.

Although the girls were good typists, white-out was at every desk, as well as boxes of carbon paper and erasers. A mistake on the original could sometimes be remedied with white-out, but every one of the seven carbon copies had to be erased and corrected by hand. The executive secretaries were the first to receive IBM memory typewriters. To have one was a status symbol, defining where the user fit in the hierarchy of importance and authority.

When we saw the need for further mechanization, we consulted with IBM, our friends at Back to the Bible, and George Wilson, who was in charge of the Billy Graham office. IBM said they would not sell us a machine unless it would be a help to our operation. George's counsel was that we couldn't afford a new machine until there was enough demand to operate it round the clock. Back to the Bible said we should convert now while we were still small. They had waited too long, and it took two years to convert.

Under Bob Siefert's leadership, we bought our first punch-card IBM machine in the early '60s. Bob held demonstrations for our crews by dumping a few hundred cards of mixed colors into the machine and showing us how rapidly it would sort them by color according to the hole punched in them.

When we upgraded years later, Jerry Bridges asked me if we should get the approval of the board of directors. I told him I didn't think so but wondered why he asked. He said the computer cost more money than it took to buy Glen Eyrie.

Lorne didn't have to spend much time supervising the office operation, but it was a real morale boost just for him to walk around among the workers. To be spoken to or touched by him would make a person's day.

Dealing with Deficit

For the first dozen years of Lorne's presidency, the headquarters administration remained about the same as what he had inherited from Dawson Trotman. The various headquarters departments, Glen Eyrie, and Eagle Lake were one entity and shared finances. The resources to support this entity came from gifts, the sale of printed ministry materials, and conference profits. We needed a minimum of $900 each working day to meet these administrative financial needs.

By early 1964, we were caught up in what was to be a cyclical trend in Navigator financial history. It looked like this: When we perceived we were overworked, we added more people without considering whether or not they would bring in the additional income needed to support them. Our expenses started exceeding our income as a result. We began borrowing to meet our financial needs and realized we had to reverse the trend posthaste.

That fall, Lorne accepted an invitation to help the Billy Graham team with counselor training in the San Francisco–area crusade. Before he left for this three-month assignment, he talked to me about our troubling financial situation, saying, "Do whatever it takes to fix it." We also discussed one of the axioms Lorne had picked up, "It is better to cut out than cut back."

I agreed. My reasoning was that if an activity was cut out but later proved to be essential, it would of necessity demand resurrection.

Paring down the office personnel was relatively easy because we had such an efficient, dedicated crew willing to do extra work. Several in supervisory roles agreed to take temporary employment elsewhere. Jerry Bridges, who supervised the office crew, moved to Kansas City to work for a paper company until finances stabilized. Others whose jobs minimized after Dawson's death also moved.

That left Glen Eyrie, with its crew of more than 40. I asked Glen Eyrie supervisor Bob Newkirk the absolute minimum number needed to keep the Glen functional. He gave me the number 28. I told him I was thinking of three, the number former owner George Strake had permanently employed. We compromised on seven. That included cook Bill Michael and his assistant so that the crews could still have their three daily meals at the Castle. But who would be cut?

First we did away with the daytime gatekeeper. Although some were horrified at the thought, we put a sign at the gate telling visitors there was a telephone directory inside and they should phone the person they came to see. We figured that everyone coming on the property came to see someone who probably knew they were coming. For the first few days, we stationed a hidden spy to observe what happened. Though some visitors seemed a little bewildered, they responded positively, and the system worked.

The next job to be eliminated was the late-afternoon and evening phone operator. We wired the phone so outside calls would ring in the men's housing. The senior staff all lived off Glen Eyrie, anyway, and the staff throughout the world knew their home telephone numbers. It worked fine.

Naturally we could not provide conference services, so all conference-related jobs were eliminated.

To our amazement, Proverbs 14:4 came to fruition—where there are no oxen the stable is clean. Within weeks, our expenses began to match our income. The January 1965 Dear Gang letter reported that we were able to pay back our $161,000 debt. Although our actions seemed a bit drastic, Lorne was happy with the outcome.

We began accumulating year-to-year surpluses that were contributed to the field ministries. This cycle of prosperity continued until 1972, when our increase in non-income–producing personnel called for repeating many of the actions taken eight years earlier.

It seems that The Navigators thrive more spiritually in adversity than prosperity. When the Lord withholds, the problem may not be finances. Instead, He may be using the shortage to call attention to the real issues He is concerned about.

The Ministry Lorne Inherited

THE GLEN EYRIE AND HEADQUARTERS functions overshadowed the Navigator field ministries that Lorne inherited in 1956. Before that, The Navigators had pretty much been where Dawson Trotman was and whatever he was doing.

When Lorne assumed leadership, The Navigators consisted of:
- 21 office staff at headquarters
- 44 field representatives, half in the United States and half overseas (3 were non-Americans)

The U.S. and Canada field ministries were made up of Navigator homes and Servicemen's Centers. There were also Navigator-manned Servicemen's Centers in Europe and Japan. A few representatives had ministries to nationals, such as Roy Robertson and a team in Japan, Jake Combs in Taiwan, and Warren Myers. Warren was a sort of missionary-at-large, having had ministries in Hong Kong, India, Vietnam, and Japan.

The Navigators also had *Topical Memory System* distribution centers in many countries, including Korea, Taiwan, Hong Kong, the Philippines, South Africa, and several European nations. These locations also sent out correspondence Bible studies, in addition to the TMS. A report in early 1957 said, "In Formosa, over 204,000 have now completed the first lesson on salvation."

In May 1957, Lorne was still absorbed in his duties with the Billy Graham crusade in New York City. I wrote to him weekly, giving an update on what we were doing at headquarters and submitting matters that needed a decision. In response to one of my letters, he wrote, "It is further impressed on my mind that the magnitude of the Navigator work is such that I must give my full time to it unless I become sort of president emeritus, letting others run the work and I just tackle other jobs—and that's certainly not on my heart to do."

Staff Conferences

At the first few staff conferences held at Glen Eyrie, the field staff was a noticeable minority. One feature of these early conferences was that the lead man or woman of every crew gave a detailed report to staff on what their job was and where they fit into the Glen Eyrie structure. I do not recall the field staff being given such a block of time. Everyone was interested in them and probably praying for them, though, so they shared the details of their ministry privately.

Under Dawson, the staff conference was pretty much a one-man show. He did everything from leading the singing to most of the speaking. Lorne continued with these responsibilities, including speaking at the closing banquet.

As the size of the conferences grew, so did the trauma. It resulted from the perception that there were too many cliques. Although I was new, there was a great deal of weeping on my shoulder. I tried to explain what I thought had happened. When a team of people do battle together, whether they win or lose, an inevitable bond is created for life. After coming to Glen Eyrie, I soon noticed that there was a camaraderie, an understanding, a closeness, acceptance, and affection among those who had fought the battle of securing Glen Eyrie together. A similar bond existed among those who had served in the Billy Graham campaigns. At staff conference, it was natural that those who had battled together banded together. They ate together and fellowshipped at every opportunity.

Although the Navigator family was exceptionally close, there were some wounded souls who felt like they were outsiders and second-class citizens. They were only healed as they banded together and bonded in new spiritual battles, of which there was an abundance of opportunity.

Eagle Lake

The original contract to purchase Glen Eyrie was between seller

George Strake and the Billy Graham organization "and/or associ-ates." When Billy decided to turn over the contract to his associate, Dawson Trotman, and The Navigators, his business manager, George Wilson, who had done the preliminary negotiating, continued in that role. One morning at breakfast during the final days of con-tract negotiating, Mr. Strake turned toward Mr. Wilson and asked, "Do you believe in Santa Claus?" Anticipating that something of a generous nature was about to take place, Wilson responded, "Yes, I believe in Santa Claus and that his name is George Strake."

Strake went on to tell him that General Palmer had acquired two 180-acre parcels in the national forest up the canyon from Glen Eyrie as water sheds for three Glen Eyrie reservoirs. (Two were never filled and remain empty today.) He had two more staked out up the canyon from Glen Eyrie. One of the two—now called Eagle Lake—had been filled as a backup to the water system at Glen Eyrie.

Mr. Santa Claus said he was going to throw in the properties as part of the Glen Eyrie deal. The only stipulation was that the valve in the dam had to be opened to recharge the Glen Eyrie reservoir at least once a year to conform to the previous water-rights agreement.

A former Glen Eyrie owner had built a small cottage on the property. He would sometimes ride his horse up Queen's Canyon to spend time there. Water had to be carried to the house from the spring feeding the reservoir. The cottage had a wood-burning cookstove. The reservoir had been stocked with fish and was a great fishing hole.

For the first few years of ownership, our maintenance crew diligently opened the valve for a few hours every year. Occasionally, some of the staff would go fishing during the day, and sometimes hardy, outdoor-loving individuals would take their own supplies and camp out overnight.

Lorne came up with the idea of using it for a boys' camp for staff children, perpetuating Dawson's interest in reaching youth. One of the early directors, Don Enright, gave the upper reservoir a real name, Eagle Lake. In the July 7, 1958, Dear Staff letter, Lorne wrote: "Eagle Lake Camp was the home for 15 junior high boys last

CHAPTER 15

week. There will be another the first week of August, and we hope to have even more camps next summer."

One summer, Lorne picked up his nephew at one of the early Eagle Lake camps and brought him home for the weekend. Always practical, Lorne told the boy to bring his suitcase to the laundry room so he wouldn't take home a bunch of dirty clothes. When they opened the suitcase, Lorne was shocked to see it was full of neatly folded clean clothes. The boy hadn't changed clothes in two weeks. When Lorne asked him why, he answered, "Nobody told me to."

The first few campers had no electricity, telephone, or running water. Communication was by shortwave radio with the antenna set up near the gatehouse. Weather changes often made communication intermittent. As the numbers of campers increased, a water tank was added, and a diesel generator installed. Tepees were erected for the campers every summer.

The two parcels were originally located as water sheds. One 180-acre parcel contained the reservoir, and the other was located a quarter-mile west across Rampart Range Road. As the U.S. Forest Service, who managed the land in between the parcels, took note of increasing activity around the lake, they proposed a swap of land to trade our isolated 180 acres for 180 acres of national forest adjacent to our lake property. They counted the number of trees on both parcels. Because they were about the same, the trade was made without any money changing hands except for our cost of recording the deed.

In the early days of the camp, there was one problem that had not been anticipated. It sometimes rained every day, and there was no indoor space for crafts or recreation. We were able to raise money and build an open-ended, A-frame building for shelter. The cost was $9,000. Anticipating it might someday be closed in, we found it would only cost $2,000 more to have it insulated, which was done during construction.

The Lord's blessing has been upon the camp from the beginning. Surrounded by the national forest, Eagle Lake campers have access to the mountains and valleys for many miles in every direction. No doubt the Lord moved Mr. Strake and the U.S. Forest Service before we even had the vision to pray about it. Thousands of boys and girls have been transformed by Christ at Eagle Lake as a result of the Lord's leading and intervention on behalf of The Navigators.

A New Promise for The Navigators

UNTIL HE COULD BE RELEASED FROM the Billy Graham team, Lorne did not get a firm hold on leading The Navigators. But with time, this man—physically shorter than most but a spiritual giant—began using his gift as an in-depth thinker to establish why God brought The Navigators into existence and what his role was to be.

Lorne was a thinker. Many times, I saw him respond to a question by saying, "I haven't thought through on that so I won't comment." (This stands in sharp contrast to many of us who have an opinion on almost any subject and have no reluctance to share it.) Lorne had concluded that the greatest premium on time is *thinking time*. He thought through a lot of things on his own, but he needed a sounding board, in addition to his wife, Lucy, as his thinking on a matter progressed.

He used his original headquarters leadership team, consisting of the department heads, as a sounding board. But after a few months, he complained to me, "I don't seem to have their full attention. They are thinking about their own departmental needs and making plans and writing notes and are not that much help to me. Apparently their department is their real identity, not being a part of my team."

Then he said, "You've had a successful career and don't seem to need the security and identity of being a department head. I want you to start getting rid of your jobs so you can be totally available to me half of your time."

I proceeded to turn over my financial responsibilities to a well-qualified man who had been assisting me in many areas, Jerry

Bridges. Eventually, Lorne asked me to transfer all of my responsibilities so that I could be available to him full time. We were back to the original six-hour conversation we had between Schroon Lake and New York City. I would fit in wherever he needed me most.

When someone asked Lorne what my job was, he would reply, "Jim does what I should do but don't want to do and what I should do but don't have time to do." He also said this about others who helped him.

When we were both at home, Lorne and I had a standing appointment at 1:30 every day for prayer, fellowship, establishing responsibilities and schedules, and making plans and decisions. How well we know another person is relative to the number and depth of shared experiences we have. It was in the nearly two decades of these meetings that I really got to know this great man.

Dawson Trotman could reduce the ministry of The Navigators to a simple, elementary concept: "Lead others to Christ and build them up to where they can repeat the process." In response to His promise in Isaiah 58:12, "Thou shalt raise up the foundations of many generations," God used Dawson to lay a solid foundation for The Navigators.

Lorne's role, though perceived as premature by some, was to build on the foundation and explode and fulfill the promise and command of Isaiah 54:3—"break forth on the right hand and on the left."

Breaking Forth

In 1963, Lorne made a significant decision that would chart the course of The Navigators.

We had invited some of our business friends to attend a two-day meeting at Glen Eyrie to advise us on the use of the Glen and the future of The Navigators. We called this group an advisory council.

As we prepared for the meeting, we became painfully aware that we didn't have a defined strategy or plans for them to evaluate. Perhaps we were just looking for affirmation in what we were doing.

A crisis loomed.

As we met to discuss it, Lorne made a decision. He said he would go up to Eagle Lake and wait on the Lord until He got word on what He wanted The Navigators to do next. Those of us on his team set up a prayer chain individually and in groups to cover him. We expected him to be gone at least a week. With great anticipation, we waited for our "Moses" to receive our "commandments" on our "holy mountain."

We were not disappointed. Three days later, Lorne returned and called us together. With great confidence, he opened his King James Bible to Isaiah 54:2–3: "*Enlarge* the place of thy tent, and let them *stretch forth* the curtains of thine habitations: spare not, lengthen thy cords, and strengthen thy stakes; for thou shalt *break forth on the right hand and on the left*"(emphasis added).

Lorne said he indeed had a word from God, and the heart of it was this: We were to enlarge, to stretch forth, to break forth on the right hand and on the left.

Throughout our history, The Navigators placed a strong emphasis on strengthening the stakes. Dawson had prayed for the world. It was now time to lengthen the cords and put a Navigator canopy over as much of the world as God directed in answer to those prayers.

Dawson Trotman's leading had been that the *fruit* of The Navigators was to be the main focus and the Navigator organization a small but necessary entity. Under Lorne, God was telling us to raise our own banner high and march with it unashamedly unfurled. By the turn of the century, it would be planted in more than 100 nations.

Lorne, along with Rod Sargent, Bob Foster, and I, presented this plan to the advisory council. We talked over plans for projects and personnel as far ahead as 10 years and tried to translate it into dollars and cents.

After this "mountaintop" event—and having put the plans supporting it in place—Lorne never looked back.

Laborers

Key to fulfilling this new command was the concept of laborers. It would be laborers who would do the work of "breaking forth" and "lengthening the cords." In a Dear Staff letter, Lorne spelled out the importance of laborers to the Great Commission and the role The Navigators would play in raising up these laborers:

"We are responsible individually and as a group and as a part of the whole Church to obey the Lord's last command—the fulfillment of the Great Commission.

"Our organizational goal, as our main contribution to the Great Commission, is to raise up laborers of many kinds, with varying capacities and gifts.

"There are three reasons for this.

"First, from the time Jesus pointed out in Matthew 9 until now, the big need is for laborers. 'The laborers are few.' We hear it from chaplains, churches, missions.

"Second, it is our historic calling, from the earliest days of Daws's prayer for 'a band of young men, strong, rugged soldiers of the cross with an eye single to His glory.'

"Third, it remains our current conviction that we can best serve the body by helping to supply its greatest need. God has renewed to us the promises which have been distinctly our own from the inception of the work—such passages as Isaiah 43:4–6, 60:22, and others."

Throughout his lifetime, Lorne often said, "In Christ's day there was a shortage of laborers. There still is today. God raised up The Navigators to do something about it."

Disciplemakers

During the three years the Sanny family lived in the Pink House (1959–1962), Lorne had a second office in the alcove off the north end of the dining room. He spent much of his work time there. It had plenty of wall space so he could post good-sized charts. Lorne believed that you had to learn how to make war on a map before you could make war on the battlefield. He frequently asked me to come over and interact with him at various stages of a project.

On one occasion, the project he was working on was how to put discipling into an organizational chart. As I looked at the chart, I noticed the word "disciplemakers," which I had never heard before.

He explained that if Christ's command to make disciples was to be obeyed, there had to be disciplemakers.

To the best of my knowledge, that word was not in the Christian vocabulary at that time. We hear it so often today we are prone to think it has been around forever. I personally give Lorne credit for coining the term.

Birthing a New Strategy

I OFTEN HEAR THE SAME QUESTION from those working to disciple others: With so many people wanting help, how do you decide who to spend in-depth time with? In answer to that question, I find myself always quoting Lorne: *"Select the ones who can help you with the others the soonest."*

This concept had wide, strategic implications as our ministry expanded around the world.

Our emerging overseas strategy came about during a two-day train trip Lorne and I made to Washington, D.C., to attend an area directors' conference. Lorne preferred to travel by train rather than fly. On the Pullman car, he would take a sleeping pill and enjoy a refreshing night's rest. (Personally, I woke up whenever the train stopped, started, or changed speed. On this particular trip, he persuaded me to take one of his sleeping pills. I am very responsive to medication, so I only took half a pill. When it was time to get up the next morning, I was so drowsy I couldn't even lift my head off the pillow.)

Lorne had brought with him a book called *The Unfinished Task* to stimulate his thinking about an overseas strategy.

We decided that the same principle we used with individuals could be applied to the nations—find the ones who could help others the soonest. We divided the world into five priority categories according to this principle:

Priority I—The United States, Canada, and Great Britain

Priority II—Northern Europe (Netherlands, Scandinavia, Germany)

Priority III—Southern Europe and Latin and Central America

Priority IV—Asia and the Pacific
Priority V—Developing nations, principally Africa

Recruiting

We had a firm grasp on our objective and our eyes on the nations, but we lacked a coherent implementation strategy. At that time, the strategy for placing staff members in new assignments was built around the idea, "Keep your bags packed and your heart open." Anyone who was part of a Navigator ministry was a potential candidate for any upcoming assignment, either domestic or overseas.

The field directors were alert for any new staff, but we had no plan for intentional, systematic recruiting. If a staff member felt called to a particular place in the world and made a convincing case, they were approved to raise financial support and proceed to the field.

A need was arising for a new faith-based plan based on a longer-term strategy. Its birth was not without labor pains.

As Lorne began sharing responsibilities with me, he told me there were probably going to be disagreements. If so, we should take a walk up the canyon to settle the matter so there would be no unsolved problem between us. Only once in 22 years did we take such a walk.

In 1960, Lorne had asked John Crawford to take a trip to Europe to evaluate our ministry among U.S. military men and women and find out how to establish a higher Navigator profile there. As a result, Bill and Shirley Greenaway were sent to oversee the military work in Europe. Shortly thereafter, Lorne asked me to be responsible for the entire overseas military ministry.

I tackled the assignment by making a survey trip to Europe, Korea, Japan, and Okinawa. In consultation with the military staff, I came up with a long-range plan to have a ministry among as many overseas U.S. military personnel as possible.

The first step was to assign priorities according to the strategic importance of the overseas military installations. The next step was to determine the number and composition of teams necessary to have the desired outcome. The third step was to recruit and establish the teams in their target areas.

Lorne was traveling away from home at the time. Copies of what became known as "The Plan" were circulated among those interested. To me, it was no big deal but simply an orderly way to tackle the assignment.

It seems that in any organization, Christian or otherwise, there is often some resentment and suspicion of the person perceived to be closest to the person at the top. It often takes the form of negative reporting. In this case, Lorne was given the impression that The Plan might be violating a sacred tradition of not getting ahead of the Lord and that the originator of The Plan—me—was usurping the prerogatives of the president.

Lorne often quoted Deuteronomy 7:22, "The LORD your God will drive out those nations before you, *little by little*" (NIV, emphasis added). This had become a principle of our organizational growth.

Lorne responded negatively to The Plan based on the feedback he was getting. He reminded me of our agreement, and we took a walk up the canyon.

We had a long discussion, with both our blood pressures at dangerous heights. We discussed how within our society, as well as The Navigators, the first reaction to a new idea is often not a reaction to the idea at all but a reaction to change. The Navigator ministry was more evolutionary than revolutionary, and conservative Lorne was cautious about change.

Another concern plagued him his entire 30 years as Navigator president. He wondered how he should reconcile what he was to do as president with the differing views of strong men he knew God had led to be on his team.

Soon after our discussion, Lorne gave full support to The Plan and enclosed a copy with his next Dear Staff letter. Soon we had recruited 26 to our overseas military staff, making it the largest-staffed region in the work at that time.

I began to receive inquiries from other Nav directors about how to recruit staff. Strategic planning was on the rise. Shortly thereafter, we developed budgets and initiated a staff retirement plan, both keys to our expansion.

One of Lorne's emerging strengths was becoming a planner and strategist, and those things would change the organization.

Fundamentals of Ministry

Throughout the late '60s and early '70s, the Navigator ministry followed Dawson's original call to reach a certain age group. These young people were found in the military and on college campuses, so that's where we had focused our energies. As Navigator alumni from both the military and the college work began to have significant ministries among adults, a new work emerged that Nav rep Chuck Singletary called Community Ministry.

The profile of an individual military or collegiate ministry in The Navigators is fairly consistent. The Community Ministry, however, sometimes strongly reflected the personality of the leader. It was also expanding so rapidly there was concern as to its Navigator authenticity.

Lorne decided we should develop a philosophy of Community Ministry. After considerable thought, he concluded that because all Navigator ministries have the same objective, what we really needed was a detailed "Philosophy of Navigator Ministry." He tackled this project with zeal greater than any I had observed since he left the Billy Graham team.

In the April 30, 1974, Dear Staff letter, Lorne wrote,

"As I attempted to work out guidelines for the fast growing Community Ministry, I realized that we need to rethink our entire ministry philosophy. We may need to make some adjustments. So we have embarked upon a study of the Bible and of our ministry experience to discover any universals that apply to the Navigator work anywhere in the world. Jim Petersen is spearheading this ambitious project."

After working on the project several months, Lorne decided he was spending too much time on it and neglecting other priorities. He asked Jim Petersen to help him full-time. With his bent toward scholarship, philosophy, and exploration, Jim was the perfect choice. He did sometimes chafe under the scrutiny of Lorne, who would not accept any segment if there was any question as to its thoroughness. Words such as "worldview" became prominent in the Navigator vocabulary during this time.

Lorne began taking the early results of the Fundamentals of Ministry (FOM) to the Europe staff in 1976. From talks with the Europe staff, he developed the FOM into a seminar and began going through it with different staff leaders throughout the world. His preoccupation with the subject led him to make a series of videotapes for Navigators worldwide. The passage most often quoted from the FOM is "evangelizing, establishing, and equipping." This is what The Navigators was about.

The FOM was later followed by the Scriptural Roots of Ministry in the 1980s and today's calling statement and core values. However, the FOM is the dictionary, the encyclopedia, the Navigator Bible, with which the authenticity of all dogma, ideas, and innovations of future Navigators can be tested. If future generations should lose the Navigator vision, perhaps a person like Josiah (2 Chronicles 34:14–21) will dust off and implement the scriptural principles found in the FOM.

Once this document was complete and made available to the staff, Lorne was content for the rest of his life to believe that an authentic Navigator ministry statement had been summarized in the three key words: evangelizing, establishing, and equipping. At that time, I felt this was perhaps the greatest legacy Lorne would pass on to future Navigators. I still do.

CHAPTER 18

Qualities of a Successful Leader

ALTHOUGH HE STARTED HIS PRESIDENCY by calling himself
the reluctant leader, Lorne did the right things and modeled successful leadership over the years. While Dawson led by the strength
of his personality, Lorne led by the strength of his character. Billy
Graham once confided to Dawson that when he recommended
Lorne to be his successor on the team, Billy was skeptical. He
wondered what it was that Dawson saw in this soft-spoken man.
He said, "It was only later that I saw how right you were and what
a great man he really is."

Reaching Agreement
To some, Lorne's style seemed to be leadership by consensus. But
Lorne did not believe that consensus leadership was biblical.

Former British Prime Minister Margaret Thatcher once said
of consensus leadership:

*"To me consensus seems to be: the process of abandoning all
beliefs, principles, values and policies in search of something in which
no one believes, but to which no one objects, the process of avoiding
the very issues that have to be solved merely because you cannot get
agreement on the way ahead."*[1]

Why then did Lorne give the impression of being a consensus
leader? Before strategic leadership meetings, Lorne and I generally
went over the issues and decided on acceptable options. Although
he was open to new light on any subject, he would skillfully guide
the discussion until there seemed to be general agreement on one

1 From a paper on leadership by Jack Mayhall.

of our predetermined options. He kept the discussion open until this was achieved. He concluded that decisions were more likely to be carried out thoroughly and enthusiastically when those affected were participants in the decision-making process.

This philosophy paid off on more than one occasion. At a 1981 meeting of divisional directors (Jack Mayhall, Doug Sparks, Jim Petersen, and me), we confronted the issue of the headquarters administrative office needing more money. Specifically, we were considering raising the amount deducted from each rep's budget. The three overseas directors opposed this, believing it was not right to decrease the reps' budgets until they could return home to do fund-raising.

Lorne wanted agreement, but we ended the day deadlocked, and he was visibly displeased. We wondered what he would say the next morning when we resumed. When we met again, Lorne opened the Bible and read from 2 Samuel 3:39, "And today, *though I am the anointed king, I am weak,* and these sons of Zeruiah are too strong for me" (NIV, emphasis added).

We got the point, had a good laugh, compromised, and moved on to the next agenda item harmoniously.

Praying Through the Day

I believe the greatest factor in Lorne's successful leadership was his practice of praying through the day backward every night.

The staff of an organization like The Navigators—as well as corporate employees and electors of political officials—are prone to overestimate the ability and capacity of the top official to correct and control all that they think should be done. It was not unusual for Lorne to come to the end of the day with a half-dozen complaints and recommendations, all of which seemed critical to their originator.

Before concluding his day, Lorne would review the day, event by event, and ask: "Lord, here is the situation. Do you want me to do anything about it? If so, what?" He would then formulate a plan of action in any area the Lord prompted him and, as a result, knew he was following the Lord's priorities.

In evaluating Lorne, his team agreed that his greatest strength was sound judgment and decision making. Paradoxically, the area in which he needed improvement was to speed up the seemingly snail-like, tedious, drawn-out, foot-dragging method by which he delayed, avoided, or made decisions. This was probably because he knew he would get the right answer from the Lord in his evening ritual.

I wonder if there may be a graveyard in heaven with monuments to the great ideas on which the Lord never led Lorne to take action.

Sticking to His Objective

Another wise leadership practice of Lorne's was staying focused on his objective. At least once every six months, Lorne and I would update and compare our job descriptions, objectives, and plans. He never changed or wavered from his objectives and priorities.

Lorne's team members were full of ideas about how to further the ministry and Lorne's best way to contribute. I can't remember the number of times I saw him pull out the board on his desk, point to his number-one objective, and say, "NO. That is not my main objective." Instead, his main objective was *to set, clarify, and maintain* the objectives of The Navigators.

One of the team members, for example, thought we should have a local radio broadcast for the Colorado Springs community. Talented George Sanchez would be the emcee and soloist, and Lorne would be the principal speaker. One glance at his objectives and Lorne said no, although he encouraged others to pursue the idea.

For the most part, Lorne followed the strategy common to corporate CEOs: Let the vice presidents run the corporation for the next five years. The president's job is to plan for year six and update every year.

Leading by Example

One of the things we appreciated most about Lorne's leadership was his commitment to lead by example. He had reservations about Christians preaching and teaching beyond their own experience. Consequently, pacesetting was very important to him.

Feeling he should be more of a pacesetter, Lorne searched out a local Navigator team that he could join in grassroots evangelism. He ended up doing barracks evangelism at Fort Carson in Colorado Springs. At that time, security was not what it is today. Navigator men in civilian clothes joined their soldier friends in contacting men in their living quarters. The first night Lorne accompanied them, someone got suspicious of this older man in the barracks and called the military police. He and the other members of the team were taken into custody and detained until midnight.

(Incidentally, Lorne and I discussed evangelism in one of our post-retirement times together. Lorne told me that he had recently asked one of Campus Crusade's top leaders what they had learned about evangelism in the past 50 years. His instant response was John 4:10—"Jesus answered her, 'If you knew the gift of God and who it is that asks you for a drink, you would have asked him and he would have given you living water'"(NIV).

Lorne reflected, "You know, if we were to start making the *Topical Memory System* over again, I don't think we would start with sin, its definition, universality, and penalty, but with a positive approach. Almost everyone knows they are sinners, are miserable in their sin, and are concerned about life hereafter. We need to start with a message of love and hope and what Christ has to give those who trust Him.")

Lorne's commitment to leading by example also spilled over into his discipling of others. Sometimes this came about in unexpected ways.

One morning, he told me he had just had a phone call from an Air Force colonel and had made an appointment to see him at 10 o'clock. The colonel told him that Ruth Graham had said he should get in touch with Lorne.

Lorne went on, "I don't know how to talk to a colonel. I will have a cup of coffee with him, we'll talk a little, and then I will bring him over to your office for you to do whatever we can for him."

I asked him for the colonel's name. He looked at the note he had made and said, "Colonel Jim Irwin."

"Do you know who Colonel Jim Irwin is?" I asked.

"No, he's just a name to me."

I told him that Irwin was one of the Apollo astronauts who had just returned from traveling on the moon in a mechanized vehicle.

"That's different," Lorne said. "But I told you I wanted you to meet with him, and that stands."

I reminded him that Ruth Graham had told the colonel to meet with Lorne Sanny, not Jim Downing. He relented, and they began to meet regularly, often by phone. Lorne got Jim started memorizing Scripture. Jim was in demand as a speaker worldwide, and more than once he told Lorne, "I used the verses you helped me memorize in one of my lectures." One of his favorite tales was that on the return journey to earth, it first looked like a small ball. But as it got bigger, the only thing he could think of was, "God so loved the world." He said that on the spot, he dedicated the rest of his life to telling the people of the world that God loved them so much He sent His only begotten Son to die for them.

In the book of Acts, we read about acts of the Holy Spirit that were carried out through the apostles. Similarly, the acts of Lorne Sanny, as he led The Navigators, were the acts of a man sensitive to the Holy Spirit's leading and direction. Lorne had followers because he was such a godly man and radiated that he was an "under shepherd" to the Great Shepherd. His most obvious drive was to obey and serve the Lord, and that's what made his leadership so successful.

CHAPTER 19

The Personal Side of Lorne

FOR 30 YEARS, LORNE MODELED the Christian life to many of us. I pass this along to you through a sampling of some big and small stories from his life.

Surrender

Lorne's message during his last months on earth was a continuation of a value he'd held throughout his lifetime—surrender.

I saw him consistently live out and preach this practice. On one of my overseas trips, I stayed with a certain staff family. The wife had experienced a recurrence of cancer, which was eventually terminal. Because he was a cancer survivor, I thought Lorne could be of special comfort to her. She had a strong inclination to claim verses related to healing. He told me that she had the wrong approach, and he wrote her accordingly. The right approach, according to Lorne, was to surrender to the will of God. (Perhaps we should all adopt this approach in our counseling instead of trying to help people who may be trying to work around what God wants to do in and through them.)

Lorne had a natural fear of flying, or should we say, a fear of "crashing and burning to death." Although traveling with him was always a privilege, driving to the West Coast or enduring a two-day train trip to Washington, D.C., seemed a high price to pay for that opportunity. Lorne realized that flying to some commitments was the best use of time, so by sheer willpower and resolve, he mustered the courage to use jet aircraft as a means of transportation. While on an extended trip overseas in 1957, Lorne wrote about flying into Nairobi in a dense fog. What happened during that hour of circling in the fog was a milestone in Lorne's spiritual life.

He said he knew Mt. Kilimanjaro was out there somewhere, and he expected to crash into it. He then recalled some of the great answers to prayer he had read about. There was the time George Mueller was en route to St. John's, Newfoundland, for an important speaking assignment. Because of heavy fog, the ship could not enter the harbor. Along with others, Mueller prayed that God would lift the fog so he wouldn't miss the meeting. Miraculously, the Lord cleared the fog, providing a great testimony to the ship's captain, crew, and passengers, as well as those anticipating his arrival.

Lorne saw himself in a similar situation. He prayed expectantly for God to lift the fog so they could land safely. But the fog didn't lift. He described the next agonizing moments, wondering why God didn't answer. The best Lorne could determine, the Lord was asking him, "Who is in charge, you or me? Who is the servant, and who is the Master? Just leave it up to me."

Lorne acknowledged His lordship, and peace filled his heart.

This did not discourage Lorne from claiming promises in the future, but it did reinforce his strong conviction about the importance of commitment and surrender. Later, Lorne remarked, "I resigned as manager of the universe, but I sometimes backslide."

He held fast to this belief through his dying days. We had several group prayer meetings with and for Lorne during the last months of his life. At one of these meetings, I quoted Jesus, who asked Bartimaeus, "What do you want me to do for you?" (Mark 10:51).

I asked Lorne, "What do you want us to unite in praying that the Lord will do for you?" He answered, "That I will have wisdom and peace." Lorne lived an entire lifetime of surrender, and even in the end, he did not ask for healing but only that the Father's will be done. His favorite verse during his final days was Psalm 31:15 (NIV), "My times are in your hands."

Burnout

During the autumn of 1968, continually being deprived of following his highest priorities, Lorne's mental, emotional, and physical fatigue caught up with him. He was forced to turn over his responsibilities to others for a three-month period.

He expressed that he even doubted his faith in God. This horrified some of the staff, which added to his frustration. He felt so under the control of others that he didn't even have the freedom to doubt. He and I didn't meet as regularly during this time so he could concentrate on recovery. My wife gave him E. Stanley Jones's book *A Song of Ascent,* which he publicly stated was a great help.

I tried to analyze what went wrong and discussed it with him. His office was in an unsatisfactory environment. He had to use the bathroom more often than most men and had to parade past an office of female secretaries at every going and coming. He had no private entrance, so everyone in the office knew when he was in and took advantage of the situation. Millie Hopkins tried to protect him, but he still felt trapped.

Those of us who were around him were negligent in not being more aware of the situation and remedying it.

When it appeared Lorne was ready to resume his responsibilities, I told him why I thought the burnout occurred and offered a possible solution. My analysis was that he went home every day feeling he had been enslaved by low-priority tasks that robbed him of the time and energy needed to accomplish the priorities the Lord had given him.

I proposed that he rent an office off Glen Eyrie and not let anyone except Millie know the location or phone number. He agreed. He had me move into his office and Millie move into my office, where she had the privacy to do her work more efficiently.

Lorne began each day at the off-site office working on his priorities. When he was ready for the routine, he phoned Millie, who would bring him the mail and relay other business matters needing his attention. Only Millie—and perhaps his family—knew the location of his office. I never went there and to this day do not know where it was. After a little more than a year, he felt ready to face the old routine and moved back into his old office.

One of the lessons I have learned in 94 years is that when we are healthy mentally, physically, spiritually, and emotionally, there is no problem or challenge to which we cannot find a solution we can live with. When we are depressed and stressed about an unsolved problem, we should look beyond the issue to find the real problem. The problem is likely that we are unhealthy in one of these areas. When our health is restored mentally, physically, spiritually, and emotionally, we can solve any problem and finally get a good night's rest (Luke 2:52).

Calling

Early in his Christian life, Lorne felt the Lord calling him to be a missionary in Latin America. He fully expected that to be his field of ministry some day. When he would occasionally mention it to others, some would try to console him by saying that he was *supervising* ministry in Latin America. His response was, "No, I feel I had a distinct call to minister there in person."

This unresolved dilemma was actually valuable in counseling staff about overseas assignments. Occasionally, when it didn't work out for a staff member who felt a strong call to a certain overseas ministry, Lorne's response was that one of two things had happened: (1) We were mistaken about the certainty of the call, or (2) The timing was for the future.

Regrets

One of the lowest points in Lorne's tenure with the Billy Graham team—and perhaps his life—came as he prepared for the Detroit crusade in 1953.

"What is the proper way to match persons coming forward at the invitation to receive Christ with a counselor?" he was asked during a counselor-training session. He recalled his 12-word answer as the most unfortunate words he ever spoke: "Men with men. Women with women. Whites with whites. Blacks with blacks."

Some in the Graham team feared they would be seen as racist and sexist and wondered how this would affect the crusade. With a lot of prayer and clarification, the furor subsided, and a successful crusade was launched.

Connecting with People

Lorne had many invitations for public speaking, and many times he was called on with little advance notice. The result was the same. He always seemed to connect with the audience and bless them in a special way.

I once said to him, "Lorne, you are the only person I know who is often called on to pinch-hit as a speaker, and when you do, you always hit a home run. What is your secret?"

He accepted the compliment graciously and said, "Well, I feel all of us are pretty much the same in the challenges we face and the struggles we are experiencing. They are common to all of us. So I just get up and talk about my personal problems and struggles and how I am dealing with them, and people seem to identify with me."

Another time when I commended him on a message, I wasn't prepared for the level of transparency in his response. He asked, "Do you know why I prepare so hard?" The reason, he said, was that so he would get feedback like I had just given him. "I doubt if I have ever done a purely objective thing in my life," he said.

Answered Prayer

Lorne had to go to London several months ahead of the 1954 Billy Graham crusade to set up the counselor training and follow-up program. That meant a long separation from his young family, particularly from his two young sons who would be left without a father's guidance. But he and Lucy committed the family to the Lord.

During his absence, Lorne's second son, Charles, age 7 at the time, and his friend were playing with a gun. They didn't realize it was loaded. The friend pointed the gun at Charles's head and pulled the trigger. Miraculously, the gun did not fire. Lorne and Lucy believed this was clear evidence the Lord was answering their prayers.

CHAPTER 19

Handling Frustrations

At the Sanny's Pleasant Valley home in Colorado Springs, the back
door was a more convenient entry than the front door. It opened
directly onto the driveway, and it seems to be a universal tendency
of visitors to park in the driveway rather than on the street. Not
many of the Sanny guests drove late-model cars. Many of the visitors' vehicles had oil leaks that marred the characteristic cleanliness
of Lorne and Lucy's residence.

To remedy this situation, Lorne bought some traffic cones and
lined them up in his driveway. They served their purpose for a few
days, until one night they disappeared.

The Sannys were great neighbors who served the community
and were highly respected. They had no enemies. Lorne had the
normal desires for acceptance and approval, and it was quite a shock
to him when the cones were removed by persons unknown. He
never replaced them and resorted to using every known chemical
for removing oil spots from his driveway.

As a popular, well-known leader, Lorne sometimes craved time
away by himself. He had a strong need to get away for rest, recupera-
tion, study, and thinking. One summer day, he took his camping
trailer to his favorite spot in the Rockies. After setting up an awning
and card table, he sat back to spend some quality time alone.

After enjoying only a few minutes of peace and quiet, a lady
came over and said, "Aren't you Lorne Sanny? We are so glad you're
here. We wondered what we were going to do for fellowship."

In retelling this story, Lorne exaggerated his response, saying he had to throw away his beer cans and share his time with
the couple.

Although Lorne was seen as unflappable, some frustrations
did affect his mood and conduct. As we got together for one of our
regular afternoon meetings, his opening words were, "Pray for me.
I have left the last three people I met with in tears."

One day just before lunch, he came rushing into my office saying, "I'm sorry, so sorry." He led me out to the parking lot where
we parked our cars side by side. He had left his office so upset that
he got into his car, revved up the engine, spun the steering wheel

to the limit, and started backing out. The problem was that he was oblivious to my car, which was parked next to his. His right front fender crashed into my parked car's left front fender, causing considerable damage to both.

We were both insured by the same company. The adjuster couldn't conceal his skepticism about Lorne's explanation as to how the accident happened.

Generosity

When I joined Navigator staff full-time in 1956, the Sannys drew the same salary as my family. The Sannys often seemed short of funds, and I sometimes wondered why they lived so frugally. Later, I discovered that they paid the monthly expenses for Dawson and Lila's son Charles, who was institutionalized after Dawson's death.

(Lorne and Lucy were no strangers to frugal living. During their first independent Navigator assignment in Seattle, they had no money for a car, so they transported their groceries home from the store in their baby carriage.)

Love

Lorne's definition of love has stood the test of time, and I quote it often: "Love is the unconditional acceptance and desire for the good of another." He offered this illustration, which tested his own commitment to love.

On the long leg of an airplane trip, Lorne's seat companion was a lady who consumed several drinks and as a result became loud and talkative. Her voice carried several rows in all directions. When she asked why Lorne wasn't drinking, he answered, "I'm a Christian and a preacher."

"Oh, I am a beautiful Christian and all that," she replied. "And do you know what I have to be thankful for?"

"Tell me," Lorne said.

"I got my tests back today, and I don't have AIDS."

He endured this conversation, shared by the other passengers, until the plane landed. This experience didn't change his definition of love, but Lorne realized he still had more work to do to live up to his own definition.

Despite what he saw as his own shortcomings, Lorne embodied love to many of the people whose lives he touched. He was once in a spiritual nurturing relationship with a young businessman from his church. As the young man was growing into a fruitful Christian, he developed terminal cancer. Lorne spent much of his time visiting the man in the hospital. As the end grew near, the man's final request was that Lorne would sit by his bed and hold his hand in his last hours on earth. Although Lorne thought it was an unusual request, he heartily responded.

Wisdom

In one of our afternoon appointments, Lorne asked, "What motivates you most?" After discussing the subject, he pulled a 5x8 card out of his desk and made a mark on it. He then showed me the card.

For several months, he had been asking people with whom he met this same question about motivation. He had six or seven answers. Each had a slash mark for the number of times he had been given that answer. The answer with by far the most marks was: "Being given something that will help me in my personal life."

A close second was: "Being given something that will help me in my ministry."

Near the bottom of the list was "Challenge."

The lasting lesson to me was a diminished view of the effectiveness of throwing out a challenge to motivate someone.

Sense of Humor

Lorne was able to observe deeply and learn from every new experience. The first of the Sanny children to be married was their oldest daughter, Beverly, whose wedding to Ted Hough took place in the Metropolitan Baptist Church in Oklahoma City. When he returned from the wedding, I said to Lorne, "You always learn from every new experience. What did you learn from the wedding?"

His response was immediate and almost gruff: "Weddings are women's affairs."

Another time, Lorne and I met with one of the staff, and the man's parting words were, "Lorne, there's a new diet out where you can lose weight and still not be hungry."

Lorne struggled with a weight problem and had more than one wardrobe to show for it. Normally so soft-spoken, he blurted out, "You're a liar."

CHAPTER 20

Retirement and Beyond

IN THE LATE 1970s, LORNE AND I sometimes discussed our futures. He fantasized that he could begin to step out of his role as president in his early 60s and that the Lord would sanction his retirement as president at 65. We both envisioned finishing our careers in a more ministry-oriented role than headquarters afforded. Two major events marked the long road toward his retirement.

In the spring of 1978, Doug Sparks and his team set up a European Congress on Disciplemaking for the European Navigators, which was held in a large hall in Düsseldorf, Germany. Approximately 3,000 European students attended the week of messages, workshops, fellowship, athletic competition, and fun. More than a thousand students from the Netherlands attended the convention and nearly that many from Great Britain. There was a United Nations–like flavor as the messages were translated simultaneously for all nationalities who attended.

It was a highlight for Lorne to be present and observe firsthand how the European collegiate ministry had prospered under his presidency. It was also a great tribute to Doug Sparks, who had established the European Navigator ministry and was in the process of stepping down from his position.

We decided to pursue the idea of Lorne changing his role to assume Doug's position as leader of the Europe ministry. But as Lorne shared the idea with various staff, he encountered strong resistance.

He told me, "As long as I keep out of sin, they will never let me step down." Later he thought of another approach and told me, "I know how to get out of the job. I will delegate my way out."

He then began to delegate the decision-making process. When a staff member would come to him for a decision, he would refer them to the person to whom he had delegated that responsibility. Despite some pressure, he would not give an inch. Gradually, the staff began to realize it was futile to consult with him on certain matters he had delegated to others.

(In the early days of his presidency, Lorne was not spared any involvement in details. On one occasion, a supervisor presented him with a job description for the man responsible for the office bathrooms. It was very detailed with tasks, timetables, names of cleaning products, and so forth. A conceptual thinker, Lorne suggested the job description read something like: "To ensure the bathrooms are clean, sanitary, and properly equipped at all times." Twenty years later, his delegating prowess had grown to the point that he refused to get involved in deciding where the new entrance to Glen Eyrie would be after the U.S. headquarters building was constructed.)

The second significant event late in Lorne's presidency came in 1981. It was on Lorne's heart to bring together as many Navigator leaders as possible from all over the world for a giant staff conference. After months of planning, Lorne reviewed the estimated cost of $400,000 and had some second thoughts. He concluded the Lord had led in the first place, and the three-week landmark gathering was held at Glen Eyrie.

As a worldwide leadership team, we agreed on the major challenges we faced and came up with plans and timetables for meeting the challenges. Lorne's newly appointed assistant, Donald McGilchrist, who had so ably served Doug Sparks, began to display his genius. He stayed up late every night summarizing the day's events in writing so we could start each new day knowing exactly where we were in our agenda.

I retired from full-time staff two years after this conference, in 1983, at the age of 70. Lorne followed in 1986. For some time, he'd had a growing sense that there were some personal objectives he wanted to fulfill but could not while consumed with his job as Navigator president. He also felt like the ministry was in good shape and that he had accomplished his objectives as president.

Lorne's retirement was a unique event in Navigator history. Dawson and Lorne had both handpicked their teams; now the opposite would happen. The team was to pick their leader. As the time came to pick Lorne's successor, the greatest need facing The Navigators was keeping a worldwide ministry of many nationalities and cultures working together harmoniously with a single vision. It would take a gifted leader to meet this challenge.

Under the Lord's leading, the staff wisely selected Jerry White, a man of tremendous strength, capacity, and gifts—and with the relational genius to continue to bond the worldwide Navigators. When Jerry stepped down from that role in 2004, the staff perceived that the greatest need was for a new emphasis on ministry practices and skills. Mike Treneer was chosen and has proven to be Mr. Ministry personified. He and his team are personally helping the Navigator world increase and maintain effectiveness in ministry.

At Jerry White's request, Lorne established the Business and Professional Ministry shortly after his retirement. Lorne had a good rapport with businessmen, and this ministry matched his gifts and motivation. Once he felt he had made his contribution in this arena, Lorne turned it over to Roger Fleming.

In 1986, Lorne began sending out *The Equipper,* an educational and motivational newsletter, to a mailing list of 3,000. Twenty-four issues were published before Lorne decided that the cost and amount of time required did not justify the results.

He also continued to minister at Navigator conferences overseas and across the United States, although he limited himself to one major conference each year.

Lorne and I sometimes discussed how we could best contribute to The Navigators in our later years. I felt that as long as the grassroots ministry of The Navigators is healthy, the Navigator ministry is healthy. It is the tail that wags the headquarters. I therefore wanted to be primarily available to and involved with the staff at that level.

Lorne chose to be available and involved with the headquarters staff. On occasion, Lorne joined me in grassroots ministry, and we had some great times. After one such occasion, he said, "I think you made the right choice."

Lorne's biggest priority after his retirement was to spend time with his family. The final decade of his life was filled with recreational activities and meals with his children and grandchildren. One highlight was taking his four daughters on a fishing trip to Montana.

What began as a shortness of breath in the late '90s was diagnosed as two tumors that were interfering with his breathing. The tumors were malignant, and he underwent treatment for the next several years, going in and out of remission. He continued coming into the office during those years, working with his secretary, Linda Geurin, with him since 1990, on correspondence and advising leaders on ministry issues when asked. He maintained a presence in the office until about nine months prior to his death on March 28, 2005, which came as a result of terminal pneumonia. In his years of illness, his main concern was not being able to care for his wife, Lucy.

During the last few weeks of his life, Lucy stayed with him during the day in the assisted-care facility. After dinner, one of his friends would stay with him until bedtime. Those of us who visited him during those days observed that there were only two items on his nightstand—his Bible and his memory pack. As his energy diminished, his faithfulness to memorize and review Scripture did not. Neither did his strong relationship with the Lord, cultivated over his entire lifetime.

Lorne's memorial service was held in the Great Hall of the Castle, the same location as Dawson Trotman's service 48 years earlier. Three hundred guests filled the Great Hall, and closed-circuit television made it possible for an overflow crowd of 200 others to view the service from the terrace. Rather than grief, the feeling was one of gratitude. When asked how many in the audience had been significantly ministered to by Lorne, at least 80 percent responded by raising their hands.

The strong testimony of Lorne's family and the renewed resolve of his friends assured us that his life had made a permanent difference for many generations to come. Lorne proved the truth of Thomas Campbell's poignant insight: "To live in the lives of those we leave behind is not to die."

PART III

Appendixes

Making Your Witness Count

BY DAWSON TROTMAN

**(Originally appeared in the
Far Eastern Gospel Crusade magazine, Spring 1953.)**

ONE SAILOR LAD WHO CAME to our Navigator home in San Pedro some twenty years ago was Jim Downing, a shrewd, skeptical youngster determined to resist the Gospel. But he couldn't resist too long the power in the lives of his shipmates on the *West Virginia*—a power that warmed and opened his heart to the Word of God, until one morning alone in a turret on the ship he quietly committed his life to Jesus Christ.

Jim has been leading men to Christ ever since. He soon found to be true something he learned from the men who brought him to the Savior and from the Book they studied—that leading a man to Christ is only a small part of the job. A man with heart prepared by the Spirit could make his decision for Christ in moments, but it was what went before and the months of patient work that followed that really counted.

What went before? The Apostle Paul described it in 1 Thessalonians 1:5: "For our Gospel came not unto you in word only, but also in power, and in the Holy Ghost, and in much assurance; *as ye know what manner of men we were among you for your sake.*" Jim did his daily work aboard ship without complaining and did it well, while non-Christians watched critically for a chink in his character. His unselfish acts and unswerving integrity added weight to the tactful word of witness that he gave. Alone on watch, Jim quietly prayed for his buddies . . . by name.

When the right time came the actual giving of the Gospel was simple. Jim usually gave a man a series of questions about the familiar John 3:16 to think over and to answer. Often, a fellow made his decision for Christ alone, as Jim had done.

Through the good seed of the Word dropped into a prepared heart, God performed a miracle of the new birth, bringing another son into His family. Instead of Jim's responsibility ending at this point, it increased. God had placed in his charge a youngster to train—he must begin to teach him how to feed on the Word, to pray, to live a Christ-centered life that would draw other men to the Savior.

Christ planned that the work of guiding the life of a young believer to maturity and fruitfulness as a disciple should be yours and mine. I am confident this is what He had in mind when He said, "Ye have not chosen Me, but I have chosen you, and ordained you, that ye should go and bring forth fruit, *and that your fruit should remain*" (John 15:16). How else could He have left in the hands of less than a dozen men the task of carrying the Gospel to all the world? The order was to go and make disciples of all nations, *"teaching them to observe all things whatsoever I have commanded you."* Impossible? No—if we apply the how as well as the what of His command.

Paul did it. Though a tireless preacher of the Gospel, ever traveling to touch new territory with the wonderful news, he constantly took time to train his Timothy . . . Titus . . . or Epaphras of Colosse . . . or Sopater . . . or Berea . . . or others who were to perpetuate and multiply his ministry in future years. This cost him time and effort, even as it had cost Jesus when He withdrew once and again from the multitudes in order to train His men in things needful for the future. There was no shortcut to making disciples.

The Thessalonian Christians reached the world in their generation (see 1 Thessalonians 1:8), and I believe with all my heart that it can be done today, if we follow Christ's order not only to evangelize but to make disciples . . . training them to reach others and in turn guide them to spiritual maturity and reproduction (Psalm 78:5, 6).

What worked for Thessalonica won't work today, some will say. But it *is* working—in Taiwan, for example, where close to 50,000 young converts are studying the Bible individually and winning their neighbors to Christ. They are not "super Christians," but simply those who have believed the Gospel and been taught how to feed themselves on the Word of God, then encouraged to pass it on to someone else. We are moving ahead on the simple principle that these babes in Christ can become the disciples that the Thessalonians were, if they are only given some of the parental care required to "disciple" them. Paul referred to this when he wrote: ". . . ye know how we exhorted and comforted and charged every one of you, as a father doth his children, that ye would walk worthy of God, who hath called you unto His kingdom and glory" (1 Thessalonians 2:11, 12).

And it worked for Jim Downing. Because he has been faithful in making disciples of the men he has led to Christ, he is an example of those who are beginning to fulfill our Lord's command to be His witnesses "*both* in Jerusalem, *and* in all Judea, *and* in Samaria, *and* unto the uttermost part" (Acts 1:8). Dave Rohrer, converted while an admiral's writer in the Navy, later headed The Navigators' work for all Europe. The Navy chief who brought him to the Lord was Don Rosenberger, who now directs the Christian Youth Crusade in Washington, D.C. Don's spiritual father, Kenny Watters, now has a responsible part in the work of Wycliffe Bible Translators, giving unreached tribes God's Word in their languages. And Kenny was one of the sailors Jim Downing reached and taught several years before on the *West Virginia.*

Thus Jim's spiritual sons of several generations are serving Christ throughout the world. While Jim served Him in the Navy, he was captain of the USS *Patapsco*, and was the self-appointed chaplain on his ship. On Sunday mornings his crew listened with respect to the Gospel message given by their firm, kindly commander who had earned their respect during the week. In over forty years of soulwinning, Jim has found it pays to attempt first to "win a hearing" for the Gospel, and to make disciples of the men who respond.

Some of us have gotten no farther than "Jerusalem" with our witness. Some have not even witnessed at home. One key to the answer is the Word. May God help us feed our own souls daily with it, live it before others as we speak it with the authority of God's messenger—and then train our babes in Christ to follow Him!

Wheel Illustration

DAWSON'S CHIEF MENTOR in his early Christian life was Pastor Vernon Morgan. Pastor Morgan felt that in order for people's Christian lives to be strong and vital, they needed ample input of the Word, a meaningful prayer life, and consistent outreach, which he called witnessing.

Morgan created an illustration using a three-legged milk stool. A person sitting on the stool had to distribute their weight evenly on the three legs for the stool to remain in balance. Pastor Morgan labeled the three legs WORD, PRAYER, and WITNESSING.

After using this illustration for a period of time, Dawson had two problems with it. He knew people who were consistent in their spiritual exercises but had such a bad disposition that it adversely affected their verbal witness. Also, the picture of a Christian in a sitting position did not agree with Dawson's concept of a Christian in action.

About 1930, Dawson created the more dynamic illustration of the Christian in action in the form of a wheel.

He added a fourth spoke called LIVING THE LIFE based on Colossians 3:23: "Whatsoever ye do, do it heartily, as to the Lord, and not unto men."

In the early days, we presented the Wheel Illustration by first having a person draw a circle representing CHRIST THE POWER, THE HUB. We then had them enclose it in a square with the circle in the center. Next we had them draw four spokes at 90-degree angles from the circle to the square, labeling them THE WORD, PRAYER, WITNESSING, and LIVING THE LIFE.

We then explained that when all four spokes were of equal length, we had a perfectly round wheel. We then personalized the illustration by having the individual put a dot on each spoke representing where they were relative to where they could and should be on each spoke. Then we had them connect the dots. Not many of the personalized wheels were perfectly round. Our point was that for a smooth spiritual ride, the four spiritual exercises had to be in balance.

The first revision came in about the seventh year of the original illustration's life. For a Christmas greeting, we on the USS *West Virginia* team decided to send our friends a greeting engraved with the Wheel Illustration.

One of our team members was the ship's photographer, so he was to create the glossy photo. To create it, he had to have a positive drawing to photograph. None of us was an artist, so we recruited one of the ship's officers to draw it for us. A problem arose. There was only room for 10 letters in each spoke, and LIVING THE LIFE has 13 letters. Dawson solved this by printing "the" in lowercase. To do so offended our officer's artistic sensibilities, and he said we would have to find another word for the spoke. Without consulting with Dawson, I substituted the nine-letter word OBEDIENCE, which I felt illustrated the same point.

When Dawson saw our glossy copy, he looked a little shocked and muttered, "Well, that's OK." It survived a few decades.

The next version was the result of a new staff member who came from a tradition where FELLOWSHIP is predominant. He made a strong case for FELLOWSHIP as a vital spiritual exercise, and a decision was made to elevate OBEDIENCE to the rim as a composite of the spokes and replace it with FELLOWSHIP.

Jim Downing's Prayer of Thankfulness for Lorne Sanny

(Given at Lorne's 1986 retirement celebration)

HEAVENLY FATHER, WE IN THE NAVIGATOR family thank you for giving gifted men and women to serve and edify the body of believers and equip them to minister to the world. We thank you for the vision you laid on the hearts of Dawson and Lila and for raising up Lorne and Lucy, who are like-minded in vision.

We thank you for Lorne's 30 years of fruitful, successful, and inspiring leadership. We thank you for Lorne's example as a man of God and for being a model as one who has challenged us in teaching, way of life, purpose, faith, patience, love, and endurance as he has been a father and pastor to us.

We thank you for his humble walk with God and selfless life. Thank you for his wise and compassionate leadership and for his foresight, wisdom, planning, and organizational skills, which have allowed The Navigators to multiply and break forth on the right hand and on the left and to expand into 62 countries of the world to minister to the people you love and for whom Christ died.

We offer thanks for Lorne's ability to discover your objectives for The Navigators, to state them clearly, and in the midst of adverse winds attempting to get us off course, to steadfastly maintain these objectives for 30 years.

Thank you for his ability to discern the signs of the times and to give us a statement of the fundamentals of the ministry to guide us in fulfilling our calling.

Thank you for Lorne's example in fulfilling the Scripture to consider others better than himself and for his persevering effort to make each of us little ones become a thousand. We thank you for his ability to delegate and to make full use of the gifts and strengths of the men of stature you send to The Navigators.

Thank you for his world vision and putting wings to his desire to get every Christian in the world into the Word and develop the ability to study the Bible for themselves.

Thank you for Lorne's pacesetting life in establishing and maintaining priorities. Thank you for his contribution to world evangelization in his ministry with the Billy Graham organization. Thank you for his example in redeeming the time. Thank you for the wise sayings he has bequeathed to us for our lives and teaching. Thank you for having Lorne teach us and demonstrate how to claim the promises you have given us.

Thank you that you are going to continue to bless Lorne and Lucy and that their greatest days are ahead as they bring forth fruit as they grow older.

Thank you in the glorious name of our Lord and Savior, Jesus Christ. Amen.

Sannyisms

- *You have to kill your snakes one at a time.*
- *You can't use the men you don't have.*
- *In responding to a compliment, "Flattery will get you anywhere."*
- *You have to work smarter, not harder.*
- *A plan is no better than the assumptions on which it is based.*
- *It is not my job to teach my children mathematics. My job is to see that they are taught mathematics.*
- *On teenagers: "Love them, feed them, and when they move out, apologize to them."*
- *The longer you live, the older you get.*
- *When asked when one was too old to work with college students, Lorne said, "When you feel too old."*
- *When older persons in his counselor-training classes complained they couldn't memorize, he responded, "If you can find your way home from this meeting without a map, you can memorize."*
- *Some people may claim to have had 30 years experience when in fact they have simply repeated the same experience 30 times.*
- *When told that Navigators were "too disciplined," Lorne observed, "We have some problems in The Navigators, but I don't think that is one of them."*